Penguin Education

Penguin Modern Psychology
General Editor: B. M. Foss

Inquiring Man
The Theory of Personal Constructs
D. Bannister and Fay Fransella

Inquiring Man
The Theory of
Personal Constructs

D. Bannister and Fay Fransella

Penguin Books

Penguin Books Ltd, Harmondsworth,
Middlesex, England
Penguin Books Inc., 7110 Ambassador Road,
Baltimore, Md 21207, U.S.A.
Penguin Books Australia Ltd,
Ringwood, Victoria, Australia

First published 1971
Copyright © D. Bannister and Fay Fransella, 1971

Made and printed in Great Britain by
Cox & Wyman Ltd,
London, Reading & Fakenham
Set in Intertype Times

Contents

Editorial Foreword

There are many different scientific strategies which psychologists use. There are some strategies of very general use. One of these is to relate the person's behaviour and experience to physical things, especially the structure and function of the nervous system and the chemistry of the body. This may be used for topics as diverse as dreaming, child development, hearing, depression, intelligence and so on. As one might expect, this approach is least useful when looking at interpersonal behaviour and the behaviour of groups, though even here there are important biochemical aspects of, for instance, dominance, submission, aggression, and of course maternal and sexual behaviour.

However, there is quite a different strategy which may have even a wider use. It is to regard man as a *categorizing* animal. All perception involves categorizing. If you see something you have never seen before you will already have categorized it as 'something I have never seen before'. At birth (and before) stimuli are categorized in the sense that the nervous system deals differently with light and sound stimuli, and so on. At the other extreme, in complex social behaviour, categorizing is very evident. A person reacts to others depending on how he has categorized them. Probably the most general dichotomous social category is 'Us versus Them'.

It is curious that there have been so few psychological systems which have used the category as the basic unit. Hayek developed one, and Tolman and Bruner used ideas of categories and the relations between them in their notions of cognitive maps and plans. But it is the American George Kelly who produced the system (with which this book is concerned) that has become sufficiently accepted to give rise to a 'school' of psychology. The theory relies on two main notions: Anticipation (or, sometimes, Prediction) and Construct. A construct is a particular kind of category, particular in that it is unique to the person using it. Two people in the same situation will construe it differently; also, for any one person, constructs may change with the passage of time, depending on the person's development, mood and so on. A person's constructs are measured by a 'repertory grid' technique invented by Kelly (and modifications of it); this has been widely used by psychologists whether or not they subscribe to personal construct theory. There is no doubt that other techniques will be developed, since it is desirable that there should be alternative ways of making such measurements. As the authors point out, construct theory does not depend on a person's ability to verbalize his constructs, but simply on an ability to make discriminations, so that it can be applied, in principle, to an unborn child. It follows of course that the theory can also be applied to non-human animals.

This book describes Kelly's theory and techniques and some of their applications. One of the authors, Don Bannister, has played an almost apostolic role in teaching and developing Kelly's ideas in Britain; the other, Fay Fransella, is highly experienced in the use of the methods, as in her rigorous and illuminating work on stuttering. The book also develops some methodological and philosophical implications of personal construct theory, as contrasted with other kinds of psychology, especially with respect to its emphasis on experience rather than overt behaviour, and the 'whole man' rather than bits of him. All this is put over with clarity and pungency. As the authors say about the book, 'Nor is it written with that bland neutrality which is the hallmark of the textbook'. Psychologists and laymen will be provoked and delighted.

B.M.F.

Preface

We wrote this book to persuade psychologists, both the formal professional kind and the informal lay kind, that personal construct theory has a massive range of implication. We have tried to explore the way in which it comments on traditional psychologies, such as 'developmental' and 'social'; on the careful personal encounter we call psychotherapy and the more adventurous personal encounter we call living; on the question of what we mean by and value in being human; on the very ambition of psychologists to create a science and the confusion attendant thereon.

It is not a textbook in that it does not attempt to cover completely either construct theory work or the aspects of psychology to which such work is relevant. Nor is it written with that bland neutrality which is the hallmark of the textbook. While attempting to give cogent grounds for our enthusiasm, our presentation of personal construct theory is avowedly evangelical, argumentative and radical.

We take the view that a theory is a working tool and not a sacrosanct creed – it is to be used, developed and ultimately replaced. It should provoke us to ask new questions while providing an orderly framework within which we can seek new answers. It should enable us to transcend the obvious.

The book is bespeckled with and occasionally awash in references and quotations because we want to show that there is a body of work and thought growing apace out of and akin to personal construct theory. We have quoted extensively from the writings of the late George Kelly because theories are not 'thrown up by the facts' or produced by professional committees – they are the product of the imagination of individual men. We hope that the quotations will show something of the quality of the man who integrated his training and experience as a mathematician, psychotherapist and academic psychologist to produce a theory which is elegant in its formal logic, precise in its methodological implications and rich in its imagination.

The book's title was chosen so as to emphasize that construct theory sees man not as an infantile savage nor as a just-cleverer-than-the-average-rat nor as the victim of his biography but as an inveterate inquirer, self-invented and shaped, sometimes wonderfully and sometimes disastrously, by the direction of his inquiries.

1 The Psychology of Personal Constructs

Firstly speak
then
begin to talk
to the you of me
and us
that is the day
we are in.
And the day is a fine gauze
and all that we are
and were seeming to be
is what we shall think on
when the bell for wakening rings.

ANNE W. GLEAVE

Currently there is a demand from many psychologists that their subject should become more 'humanistic'. This is comical in one sense – it is as if sailors suddenly decided they ought to take an interest in ships – but necessary in another. A variety of vanities have diverted psychologists from concern with whole men. A craving to be seen as scientists has led them to favour a model of miniscule man. Only thus could they justify mimicking the procedures of the natural sciences in such a concretistic manner. A desire to maintain a separateness from their 'subjects' with the balance of expertise clearly in the psychologists' favour has led them to elaborate and maintain de-humanizing mysteries. Once a profession of 'psychologist' was established it was deemed necessary to find models of man which would sharply distinguish the professional psychologist from his object of study, the 'organism'.

Such idealized distinctions between scientist-psychologist

and organism-subject have a dreamlike quality. Laing (1967, pp. 15–17) points up the paradox thus:

The other person's behaviour is an experience of mine. My behaviour is an experience of the other. The task of social phenomenology is to relate my experience of the other's behaviour to the other's experience of my behaviour. Its study is the relation between experience and experience: its true field is *inter-experience*. . . . I cannot experience your experience. You cannot experience my experience. We are both invisible men. All men are invisible to one another. Experience is man's invisibility to man. Experience used to be called The Soul. Experience as invisibility of man to man is at the same time more evident than anything. *Only* experience is evident.

Experience is the *only* evidence. Psychology is the logos of experience. Psychology is the structure of the *evidence,* and hence psychology is the science of sciences. . . . Natural science is concerned only with the observer's experience of things. Never with the way things *experience us.* That is not to say that things do not react to us, and to each other.

Natural science knows nothing of the relation between behaviour and experience. The nature of this relation is mysterious – in Marcel's sense. That is to say, it is not an objective problem. There is no traditional logic to express it. There is no developed method of understanding its nature. But this relation is the copula of our science – if science means *a form of knowledge adequate to its subject*. The relation between experience and behaviour is the stone that the builders will reject at their peril. Without it the whole structure of our theory and practice must collapse.

The cardinal quality of personal construct theory is its recognition that psychology is man's understanding of his own understanding. By making its model man 'man the scientist-psychologist' it presents us with a framework which is cousin to history and poetry, while embodying the kind of systematic attack, public definition and experimental articulation which are the universal aspects of science. It is a psychological theory which admits that values are implicit in all psychological theories and takes as its own central concern the liberation of the person.

What is not a theory?

In every scientific discipline bar psychology, workers seem to accept the idea that their science will advance in terms of the building, the testing and the elaborating of theories. In psychology, many of us behave as if 'theory' were like heaven – a fine place to go when the practical business of living is all over, but not a matter of much concern here and now. We manifest our contempt for theory by using the word indiscriminately. Hence the need to begin by specifying what a theory is not.

A theory is not a notion

Consider for example 'cognitive dissonance theory' (Festinger, 1957) – this is the argument that an individual strives to reduce cognitive dissonance and to achieve consonance. Ideas or actions are considered dissonant if one implies a negation of the other, as in a person believing one thing and doing another or holding mutually contradictory attitudes. Now this is clearly a notion. It is the sort of idea which coffee-table conversation amongst psychologists might produce and, historically, a fairly large number of experiments have been attached to this particular idea. But it is still a notion, not a theory. It is simple and vague and its very simplicity and vagueness have facilitated *ad hoc* operational definitions and the multiplication of experiments – Chapanis *et al.* (1964) give detailed argument for this assertion. But it lives on, a small, impoverished thing, which can only be stuck to other notions by the glue of common sense, *ad hoc* argument and arbitrarily assembled concepts. Cognitive dissonance and kindred notions ('n-ach', 'response style', 'arousal' and so forth) function in psychology much as folk tales function in literature. Just as a folk tale can form the plot basis for endless plays and novels, so a proverbial idea like cognitive dissonance can form the plot basis for endless experiments. But it is a notion, not a theory, it cannot be elaborated into a theory and the experiments done in its name are ultimately unrelatable to the countless others done to equally plausible prescriptions.

The term theory should be reserved for extensive and elaborate systems of ideas cast in terms of an integrated language such that users do not have to borrow, in every intellectual emergency, from elsewhere and conclude by assembling a ragbag of concepts which cannot be cross-related. It should be reserved for such formalized structures of ideas that have a wide *range of convenience* such that they may ultimately explain much that is not even envisaged at the time they are constructed. Yet always the explanations must be derivable from, and relatable to, what has gone before.

A theory is not a dogma

A common objection to theories among psychologists stems from the belief that they are limiting, blinkering and imprisoning devices. This belief confuses theory with dogma. A religious or moral dogma is something that it is proposed we live by – a scientific theory is something that it is proposed we live with and explore. In the case of dogma we may cherish and defend it, in the case of a scientific theory we should cherish and attack it. Scientific theories must be regarded as expendable. They are designed to be tested to the limit and beyond. Far from blinkering they should liberate in the sense that they formulate new issues for us to consider, new pathways for us to explore – issues and pathways which would not be available had not the theory pointed them out.

The kind of psychologist who sees theory as enslavement usually sees empiricism and eclecticism as a kind of freedom. But the near-mindless collection of data and the promiscuous attachment to whatever stray concepts happen to be around in times of need, is not freedom. It is a lack of point and direction. Kelly (1955) said on this issue of theory and freedom: 'Theories are the thinking of men who seek freedom amid swirling events. The theories comprise prior assumptions about certain realms of these events. To the extent that the events may, from these prior assumptions, be construed, predicted and their relative courses charted, men may exercise control, and gain freedom for themselves in the process' (vol. 1, p. 22).

A theory is not an explanation of some 'thing'

Just as the micro-theory is a contradiction in terms, so even an extensive system of explanation that ties itself specifically to a particular concept-phenomenon is not a theory. Thus, psychology is encumbered with theories of 'language' or theories of 'memory' or theories of 'motivation'. In each case the intellectual effort is ultimately infertile because it accepts the boundaries of the concept – the 'thing' which it set out to explain. A theory of 'memory' can be no better than the concept of 'memory' itself. Someone who has accepted the concept of 'memory' so completely that he will build a theory in its name, is unlikely to find out just how limited the concept is. This is the sickness of chapter-heading psychology which has made a textbook convenience the limits of our imagination.

A true theory must be stated at a very high level of abstraction. It must be, in a practical sense, without content so that it can be elaborated and thus escape the limited categories that lay thinking has bequeathed to us. A true theory must define its own form – it must in effect delineate *psychology*.

Characteristics of construct theory

There are several respects in which construct theory may seem strange to those encountering it for the first time.

Firstly, it is presented as a complete, formally stated theory. This is very unusual in psychology, where theories tend to be stalactitic growths, which have accumulated over the years (often with later accumulations contradicting earlier ones). It would be a brave and foolish man who said he knew exactly what 'learning theory' was or what 'Freudian theory' was. Construct theory was put forward in a complete, elaborate and formal statement by one man at one time (Kelly, 1955). Although experiments, arguments and interpretations have built up around the theory, it is still possible to state its central tenets in an orderly and complete fashion.

Secondly, the theory is reflexive – personal construct theory is an act of construing which is accounted for by personal construct theory. Putting it another way, it does not, like learning theory, account for all kinds of human behaviour *except* the formulation of learning theory – construct theory treats scientists as men and, for that matter, men as scientists. 'There may be no onus on the chemist when he writes his papers on the nature of acids and alkalis to account in terms of his acid-alkali distinction for his behaviour in writing a journal paper. But psychologists are in no such fortunate position' (Bannister, 1966a). One of the effects of this is to make the model man of personal construct theory look recognizably like you: that is, unless you are the very modest kind of man who can see himself as the stimulus-jerked puppet of learning theory, the primitive infant of psychoanalytic theory, or the perambulating telephone exchange of information theory. If you do not recognize yourself at any point in personal construct theory, you have discovered a major defect in it and are entitled to be suspicious of its claims.

Thirdly, construct theory was deliberately stated in very abstract terms to avoid, as far as possible, the limitations of a particular time and culture. It is an attempt to build a theory with a very wide range of convenience, a theory not tied to one particular concept-phenomenon. It is not a theory of some 'thing': of 'learning', of 'interpersonal relationships', of 'development'. It is a psychology of man as a person, with all that is thus implied. At first reading the theory often seems dry because it is deliberately content-free. It is the user of the theory who has to supply a content of which the theory might make sense. Kelly had particular terrains which concerned him, such as the understanding of the processes going on in psychotherapy, but he sought to make his theory comprehensive enough to serve the purposes of those with very different issues in mind.

Finally, the theory does not have its philosophical assumptions buried deep inside it, it has them explicitly stated. Kelly (who dearly loved contriving a fine bit of terminology) gave the label of *constructive alternativism* to these philosophical assumptions and argued them at some length. At one point he summarizes them thus:

Like other theories, the psychology of personal constructs is the implementation of a philosophical assumption. In this case the assumption is that whatever nature may be, or howsoever the quest for truth will turn out in the end, the events we face today are subject to as great a variety of constructions as our wits will enable us to contrive. This is not to say that one construction is as good as any other, nor is it to deny that at some infinite point in time human vision will behold reality out to the utmost reaches of existence. But it does remind us that all our present perceptions are open to question and reconsideration and it does broadly suggest that even the most obvious occurrences of every-day life might appear utterly transformed if we were inventive enough to construe them differently.

This philosophical position we have called *constructive alternativism* and its implications keep cropping up in the psychology of personal constructs. It can be construed with the prevalent epistemological assumption of *accumulative fragmentalism*, which is that truth is collected piece by piece. While constructive alternativism does not argue against the collection of information, neither does it measure truth by the size of the collection. Indeed it leads one to regard a large accumulation of facts as an open invitation to some far-reaching reconstruction which will reduce them to a mass of trivialities.

A person who spends a great deal of his time hoarding facts is not likely to be happy at the prospect of seeing them converted into rubbish. He is more likely to want them bound and preserved, a memorial to his personal achievement. A scientist, for example, who thinks this way, and especially a psychologist who does so, depends upon his facts to furnish the ultimate proof of his propositions. With these shining nuggets of truth in his grasp it seems unnecessary for him to take responsibility for the conclusions he claims they thrust upon him. To suggest to him at this point that further human reconstruction can completely alter the appearance of the precious fragments he has accumulated, as well as the direction of their arguments, is to threaten his scientific conclusions, his philosophical position, and even his moral security. No wonder, then, that, in the eyes of such a conservatively minded person, our assumption that all facts are subject – are wholly subject – to alternative constructions looms up as culpably subjective and dangerously subversive to the scientific establishment (Kelly, 1970a, pp. 1–2).

Kelly is here asserting that we cannot contact an interpretation-free reality directly. We can only make assumptions about what reality is and then proceed to find out how useful or useless these assumptions are. This is a relatively popular contention in modern philosophy and many psychologists would pay at least lip service to it. However, in much psychological writing there is a noticeable tendency to revert to the notion of a reality whose nature can be clearly identified. Hence the use of the term 'variable' as in the phrase 'variables such as intelligence must be taken into account'. 'Intelligence' is a dimension which man has invented and in terms of which he can construe other men. It is not a *thing* which *must* be taken into account. Entirely different constructions can be used which do not involve such a dimension at all. In our schooldays we recognized constructive alternativism when we used to write our history essays in terms of the *political, religious* and *social* aspects of a particular period. However, even then there was a tendency to start and talk about political, religious and social 'events' as if these were really separate events, rather than various ways of construing the same events.

This approach has clear implications for the great *free will* versus *determinism* debate. One of them is that *free-determined* is a construction we place on acts and it is useful only to the extent that it discriminates *between* acts. To say that man is entirely determined is as meaningless as to say that he is entirely free. The construction (like all our interpretations) is useful only as a distinction and even then the distinction must have a specific range of convenience. A person is free *with respect to* something just as he is determined *with respect to* something else. In this way construct theory avoids the determinist argument that puts the arguer in the paradoxical position of being a puppet *deciding* that he is a puppet. For that matter how many scientists who say that they are determinists sound like determinists when they are describing the glories of scientific method. They extol a deliberate manipulation of the universe in order to explore (note the teleology) its nature. Equally, construct theory avoids the doctrine of unlimited free will which suggests a mankind that cannot be understood because it has no 'cause and effect' aspects. In contrasting his approach with that of Freudians (you are the victim of your infancy) and behaviourists (you are the victim of your reinforcement schedules), Kelly argued that man is not the victim of his autobiography though he may *enslave himself* by adhering to an unalterable view of what his past means. Thereby he fixates his present.

From this same standpoint Kelly rejects 'hydraulic' theories of man – theories which postulate some 'force' (motive, instinct, drive) within man, impelling him to movement. He argues (Kelly, 1962) that it is entirely unnecessary to account for movement in a theory which makes movement its central assumption. Thus he says: 'Suppose we began by assuming that the fundamental thing about life is that it goes on. It isn't that something *makes* you go on; the going on *is the thing itself*. It isn't that motives *make* a man come alert and do things; his alertness is an aspect of his very being.'

In the light of this approach we can see that Kelly is not proposing personal construct theory as a contradiction of other psychological theories, but as an alternative to them – an alternative which does not deny the 'truths' of other theories, but which may provide more interesting, more inspiring, more useful and more elaboratable 'truths'.

The formal structure of personal construct theory

The central tenets of the theory are stated in the form of a fundamental postulate and eleven elaborative corollaries.

Fundamental postulate: *a person's processes are psychologically channellized by the ways in which he anticipates events.*

This implies many things – it implies that man is not reacting to the past so much as reaching out for the future; it implies that a man checks how much sense he has made of the world by seeing how well his 'sense' enables him to anticipate it; and it implies that a particular man is the kind of sense he makes of the world. The word 'anticipates' is nicely chosen because it links the idea of prediction with the idea of reaching out and beating the world to the punch.

The fundamental postulate is Kelly's attempt to state what man is in business for. Just as other theories have assumed that man is in business to process information or to adapt to his environment or to reduce his drives or to obtain wish-fulfilment, so Kelly stresses that man is in business to make sense out of his world and to test the sense he has made in terms of its predictive capacity. Thus, the model man of construct theory is 'man the scientist'. This picture of man as striving for personal meaning is elaborated in the following corollaries.

Construction corollary: *a person anticipates events by construing their replications.*

The dinner we ate yesterday is not the same dinner that we ate today, but our use of the construct *dinner* is an explicit recognition of some sameness, some replication, which we wish to affirm. Thus, basic to our making sense of our world and of our lives, is our continual detection of repeated themes, our categorizing of these themes and our segmenting of our world in terms of them. Kelly often used the analogy of listening to music to illustrate this corollary, because it allowed him to stress that the replication is something which emerges because of our interpretation. Each time we hear a melody played in a piece of music, different instruments may be used, there may be a change of key, there may be a change of rhythm and so forth, but still we recognize the replicated theme. At a very basic level the themes we recognize, the samenesses we detect, can be 'concrete', as in our noting new examples daily of *pencils* and *sneezes* and *shoelaces,* or they may be very complex, subtle and highly personal replications, as when we realize that once again we have met *defeat* or *affectation* or *truth.*

Kelly is here aiming to make every assumption clear, to reach down to the obvious which must be stated if a theory is to be built up in an explicit manner. Thus, our capacity to recognize replicated themes is an explicit assumption of the idea of conditioning. Yet it is not dealt with in conditioning experiments because the experimenter gives the status of 'reality' to the generally recognized replications on which he bases his investigation. For example, we might attempt to condition an eyeblink response to the stimulus 'prime number' by blowing a puff of air into the eye of the subject every time a prime number is flashed on a screen, but not when a non-prime number is flashed on a screen. Whether we succeed in establishing such a conditioned response will depend on whether the construct *prime number* versus *non prime number* exists in the personal construct system of our subject. If it does not, he might condition to replications that he can perceive. For example, he might establish a conditioned response to odd numbers because prime numbers, bar two, are always odd. (The experience for him would then have become an intermittent reinforcement study.) But no matter how many conditioning trials he experiences, the presentation of yet a new prime number will not elicit the conditioned response. The presentation of the same prime number many times might establish a conditioned response to that particular prime number, but not to the replicated theme of primeness.

The fallacy of stimulus-response psychology (and its more sophisticated derivatives) is that a man responds to a stimulus. He responds to *what he interprets the stimulus to be* and this in turn is a function of the kind of replications (constructs) he has detected in or imposed upon his universe. Thus, Humphrey pointed out that you can condition (by electric shock) a man to withdraw his arm when the note G is played on the piano, but when you play him 'Home Sweet Home' he will not twitch a muscle, although the tune contains the note G fourteen times. Presumably because he construed it as a 'tune' and not as a series of notes (see, for example, Humphrey, 1933, p. 237).

Individuality corollary: *persons differ from each other in their construction of events.*

It could be argued that the fundamental mystery of human psychology is covered by the question 'Why is it that two people in exactly the same situation behave in different ways?' The answer is of course that they are not in the 'same' situation. Each of us sees our situation through the 'goggles' of our personal construct system. We differ from others in how we perceive and interpret a situation, what we consider important about it, what we consider its implications, the degree to which it is clear or obscure, threatening or promising, sought after or forced upon us. The situation of the two people who are behaving differently is only 'the same' from the point of view of a third person looking at it through his particular personal construct goggles.

Among the many implications of this statement is that when people are said to be similar, it is not necessarily because they have had the same experiences, but that they have placed the same interpretations on the experiences they have had. Two bank clerks may work at adjoining counters and live what are, in terms of concretely accounted stimuli, very 'similar' lives, but they may be entirely unable to make sense out of each other. On the other hand, one of the bank clerks may correspond with an aged missionary working out his life's significance in the jungles of some tropical country. These two may find their exchange of letters full of meaning, because they have basic similarities in their way of construing events. This corollary does not argue that men never resemble each other in their construing (the later sociality and commonality corollaries cover this) but it does argue that in the final analysis none of us is likely to be a carbon copy of another. Each of us lives in what is ultimately a unique world, because it is uniquely interpreted and thereby uniquely experienced.

Organization corollary: *each person characteristically evolves, for his convenience in anticipating events, a construction system embracing ordinal relationships between constructs.*

The term 'system' in the phrase 'a personal construct system' directly implies that a person's constructs are inter-related and in this corollary Kelly is stressing that the relationship is often one of inclusion or subsuming. For some people the construct *traditional jazz* versus *modern jazz* may be subsumed as a subordinate implication of the construct *good jazz* versus *bad jazz* and both poles of the construct might be subsumed under the 'music' end of the construct *music* versus *noise*. This hierarchical quality of construct systems is what makes our world a manageable place for us. The simple trick of grouping hundreds of different ways of making a living under the construct *jobs* (versus *hobbies* or versus *rest* or versus *vocations*) means that we can then handle a whole range of such subordinate constructions easily. We can offer them to each other, look at their higher, more superordinate implications, add to the category when necessary and so forth. A further way of regarding this corollary and evaluating it is given in the following terms by Bannister.

This pyramidal structure of construct systems seems to serve a variety of purposes in science and in living. For example, if we accept that the more superordinate constructs will have more implications and a wider range of convenience than their subordinate constructs, then 'climbing up our system' may be a way of finding strategies for cross-referring more subordinate constructions which cannot be directly related to each other 'across' the system. Thus the old adage that you can't add *horses* and *cows* is nonsense as soon as you climb up the subsystem and subsume them both as *farm animals* and you can blithely add in *hermit crabs* if you are prepared to climb up as far as *forms of organic life*.

Equally you may use the hierarchy as a conflict-resolving process by taking decisions in terms of the most superordinate, relevant construct. For example, for some of us *courteous–discourteous* may be a subordinate construct to *kind–unkind* and if this is so, we may in exceptional circumstances decide to be *discourteous* if we feel that in the long run this is the *kindest* way to be (say in curtailing a mutually disastrous relationship). However, if that is the way we organize our constructs, then it would not make sense for us to be *cruel* in order to be *courteous*. Going down the pyramid if we assume that for us *spitting in the spittoon–spitting on the carpet* is a subordinate construction (one possible operational definition if you like) of the construct *courteous–discourteous* then again, in exceptional circumstances (say in a culture which has reversed our particular rituals), we may find it makes sense to *spit on the carpet* in order to be *courteous* (Bannister, 1970a, p. 57).

Dichotomy corollary: *a person's construction system is composed of a finite number of dichotomous constructs.*

Kelly is here arguing that it is more useful to see constructs as having two poles, a pole of affirmation and a negative pole, rather than see them as concepts or categories of a unipolar type. In line with his philosophy of constructive alternativism he is not asserting that constructs *are* bipolar, and that they are *not* unipolar. He is merely asserting that we might find it more useful to think about them *as if* they were bipolar. Most people recognize bipolarity where it has an explicit verbal label to cover it – *black* versus *white*, *up* versus *down*, *nice* versus *nasty, here* versus *there, concrete* versus *abstract, noisy* versus *quiet, intelligent* versus *stupid, male* versus *female* and so forth. However, Kelly asserts that even where there is no label readily available for the contrast, we do not affirm without implicitly negating *within a context*. There would be little point in asserting that 'I am tired' if the contrast assertion of freshness and energy were not implicitly around somewhere to be negated. When we point and say 'That is a chrysanthemum', we are not distinguishing it from every other object in the universe, we are usually contrasting it with some other flower it might have been confused with, i.e. this is what we are doing *psychologically*, whatever the logicians say we are doing *logically*.

The idea of bipolarity in constructs also allows us to envisage a variety of relationships between them – they can be correlated or logically interrelated in many ways, whereas concepts can only either include or exclude one another. There seems a tendency to think of Kelly as an illiberal person who was trying to plead for a black and white world in which there were no shades of grey. In fact, Kelly insisted that constructs could be used in a *scalar mode*, while still being bipolar in origin. Thus, the famous 'shades of grey' stem from the construct *black* versus *white*. It is interesting to note that in terms of choice and decision we invariably break back from scalar modes of construing (which are most useful when we are speculating about and investigating a problem) to bipolar modes of construing. We may spend a long time, if we have to get the piano through the door, in measuring, in most exquisite scalar mode, all kinds of dimensions, but eventually we have to decide that the bloody thing will either go through or it will not.

People sometimes seem to think of constructs as double ended categories with fixed contents. Kelly stressed that they are portable *axes of reference*. Thus, North–South is a useful distinction but clearly Timbuctoo can be either North or South depending on where you are; the construct is not a 'container' for North 'things' and South 'things'.

Choice corollary: *a person chooses for himself that alternative in a dichotomized construct through which he anticipates the greater possibility for the elaboration of his system*.

This is the corollary whereby Kelly tucks the tail of his theoretical snake into its mouth. He thereby creates either a tautology or a complete and integrated theory.

If man is in business to anticipate events and if he does this by developing a personal construct system, then he will move in those directions which seem to him to make most sense, i.e. to elaborate his construct system. Kelly pointed out that the elaboration may take the form of definition (confirming in ever greater detail aspects of experience which have already been fairly actively construed) or extension (reaching out to increase the range of the construct system by exploring new areas that are only very partially understood). It must be stressed, however, that the elaboration is sought in terms of the system as it exists at the time and that the choice corollary does not imply that we always successfully elaborate. We can over-define to a point where we suffer the death of ultimate boredom, circling in a ritual manner around the same area, or we can overreach the system and suffer death by ultimate chaos. It has been argued (Holland, 1970) that this corollary is untestable and in that sense unscientific. It can be counter-argued that the corollary is testable if we know enough about the structure of a particular individual's system to predict his choices in terms of that system.

Range corollary: *a construct is convenient for the anticipation of a finite range of events only.*

This follows from the original assertion that constructs are bipolar and finite in number. Kelly is here stressing that he is not simply refurbishing the old notion of a concept. The *concept* of 'furniture' as a general abstraction includes tables, chairs, desks, commodes and so forth and contrasts with *everything* that is not included in the category of furniture. The *construct* of 'furniture' as used in a *particular context* would include tables, chairs and so forth *as contrasted with* say office equipment, or *as contrasted with* Georgian tables which are to be regarded as objects of art. The whole construct would then *exclude* sunsets, battleships, acts of heroism and candyfloss which are outside the *range of convenience* of the construct; they are not subsumed under either pole of it.

Kelly used the term *focus of convenience* to indicate those things for which a construct was specifically developed. Thus, the construct 'honesty', for some people, has as its *focus of convenience* keeping your fingers off other people's property and money. The focus of convenience of construct theory is the psychotherapeutic situation. The *range of convenience* is all those things to which people might eventually find the construct applicable; thus for some people 'honesty' can eventually be used in relation to political honesty, sexual honesty, aesthetic honesty and so forth. In later sections dealing with grid method, it will be seen how the range corollary, along with the dichotomy corollary and others, guides the construction of the instrument, which in its turn, provides operational definitions for some of the constructs of the theory.

Experience corollary: *a person's construction system varies as he successively construes the replication of events.*

This is the developmental focus of the theory and obviously relates to the choice corollary. A personal construct system is not a collection of treasured and guarded hallucinations, it is the person's guide to living. It is the repository of what he has learned, a statement of his intents, the values whereby he lives and the banner under which he fights. A personal construct system is a theory being put to perpetual test. Thus, one man may construe *private* versus *exposed* as aligned with *safe* versus *dangerous*, and live in these terms until other aspects of his construction system force him to risk the dangers of 'exposure'. If he then does not experience the penalties of 'danger', the link between these constructions may be weakened and that aspect of the system begin to modify. Systems flow and modulate continuously, as do the theories of scientists, but as will be shown in relation to constructs such as 'hostility', we do not modulate invariably or always logically.

Construct systems change in relation to their varying validational fortunes, predictions are sometimes proved correct, sometimes found wanting. This central aspect of the theory has been described by Bannister in the following terms.

The constructions one places upon events are working hypotheses which are about to be put to the test of experience. As our anticipations are hypotheses to be successively revised in the light of the unfolding sequence of events, a construction system undergoes a progressive evolution. The constant revision of personal construct systems is a function of incoming varying validational experience. Constructs are essentially *predictive*. Thus, when we construe a man as *honest* rather than *dishonest* we are essentially predicting that if we lend him money we shall get it back. When we construe a table as *solid* rather than *liquid* we are essentially predicting that if something is placed upon it it will stay 'on the surface' and not 'be submerged'. Constructs are not merely ways of labelling our universe, they are ways of trying to understand and anticipate it. Since every act of construing is simultaneously an act of prediction it follows that every act of construing may have one of three outcomes. The elements (objects, persons or whatever) which we construe as X may turn out to be X and we are validated. The elements may turn out to be the opposite of X and we are invalidated. The elements may turn out to be outside the range of convenience of our construct X-not-X. Thus, when the hopeful young man takes the young lady back to his flat he may construe her as *willing* rather than *unwilling* and he may be validated – an affair commences. He may be invalidated – she slaps his face and rings for the police. The element may turn out to be outside the range of convenience of the construct – 'she' turns out to be a transvestite. It is precisely because constructs are essentially predictions that our construct systems are in a continual state of change for each of us. As the evidence comes in we tend to modify the individual construct or parts of our construct system. The modification may be a minor one. We may simply shuffle the element from one pole of the construct to the other. A person we regard as *loving* behaves nastily and we now proceed to regard him (construe him) as *hating*. However, we may be wrong so persistently that we have to make some more major alteration, such as dispensing with the construct *loving–hating* and developing some other construct to view the element through. Or we may have to modify whole subsystems within our construct system in order to get a truer (more predictive) view of the elements which confront us (Bannister, 1966b, p. 366).

Modulation corollary: *the variation in a person's construction system is limited by the permeability of the constructs within whose range of convenience the variants lie.*

Kelly's theory is a theory of change. He argues that man is a 'form of motion' not a static object which is occasionally kicked into movement. However, he is at pains to suggest parameters for change, and the modulation corollary is such a parameter. The construct *permeable – impermeable* refers to the degree to which a construct can assimilate new elements within its range of convenience, generate new implications. Some constructs are for most of us fairly impermeable – we happily apply *fluorescent* versus *incandescent* to sources of light, but rarely find its range of convenience extendable. On the other hand, for most of us a construct such as *good* versus *bad* is almost continually extending its range of convenience. When we are faced by a 'new' situation then, if we generally traffick in permeable constructs, we can use them to make sense out of the new events which confront us. If our constructs tend to be impermeable, then we may take pains to make sure that we do not encounter 'new' situations, or else we may force them into the existing system however bad the fit. Both permeable and impermeable constructs are useful in given contexts, but the corollary stresses that one of the dangers of being too precise is that it transfixes one to a particular precision.

Fragmentation corollary: *a person may successively employ a variety of construction subsystems which are inferentially incompatible with each other.*

Kelly is here suggesting a further parameter of change – a parameter that suggests that change is not and need not be 'logical' in the simple sense of that term. A construct system is a hierarchy and also a series of subsystems having varying ranges of convenience. Therefore, conclusions about the 'same' series of events can be drawn at levels which are not necessarily consistent with or even related to each other. This is elaborated by Bannister and Mair in the following terms.

Although the presence of permeable constructs may allow the variation of aspects of a person's construct system to accommodate new evidence, this does not mean that a person's system will be completely logically related, with every construct being implied by every other one. The way a person will behave today cannot necessarily be inferred from the way he behaved yesterday. A parent may kiss and hug a child at one moment, smack him a little later and shortly afterwards ignore him when he insists on showing off by excessive chattering. To the casual observer, it may seem that one response could not be anticipated from the previous one and that grossly inconsistent behaviour and constructions were being adopted by the parent. This may be the case, but need not be so. Just because different constructions do not seem consistent with each other and one cannot be inferred from the other directly, it does not mean that no consistency exists for the person involved or for some other observer of the scene. When, for example, the parent's *super-ordinate* constructs concerning love and training are considered, some thread of consistency in the various actions may be noted (Bannister and Mair, 1968, p. 22).

Commonality corollary: *to the extent that one person employs a construction of experience which is similar to that employed by another, his processes are psychologically similar to those of the other person.*

This is the converse of the individuality corollary and stresses that people are not similar because they have experienced similar events; nor for that matter similar because they appear, along some limited time line, to be manifesting similar behaviour; nor yet again similar because they utter the same verbal labels. People are similar because they construe, i.e. discriminate, interpret, see the implications of events, in similar ways. They are similar in so far as, and with respect to, events which have the same meaning for them. This is an interesting corollary in its implications for experimental psychology, since it implies that we do not need to put people into the 'same' experimental situation in order to find out whether they are similar or different. People in the 'same' situation may be behaving similarly for the time being, but attaching a very different significance to the events they are encountering and to their own behaviour. Any long term predictions we make as to the continuance of their identity, on the basis of this temporary behavioural similarity, are likely to lead us very much astray. On the other hand to the degree that we can explore and evaluate the personal construct systems of two people, we may be able to determine similarities between them, having observed them in apparently different situations.

Sociality corollary: *to the extent that one person construes the construction processes of another, he may play a role in a social process involving the other person.*

This is a key corollary in that it is Kelly's attempt to explain why we bother with each other at all. It insists that interpersonal interaction is in terms of each person's understanding of the other. This is quite different from assuming that people can only interact when they have similar construction systems or are in some sense similar people. An adult may interact for a long time with a child and be very much playing a role in a social process with that child. This does not imply that his construct system is the same as the child's, only that this construct system gives him a meaningful picture of the child's construct system. Nor does it make role a purely social construct, that is, see it as the acting out of a dialogue written for the two persons by the society in which they have been brought up. It sees each of us as attempting, in relation to other people, to be psychologists, whether we be good, bad or indifferent psychologists. In terms of our ideas about the other person's construct system we may seek to inspire the other person, confuse him, amuse him, change him, win his affection, help him to pass the time of day or defeat him. But in all these and many other ways we are playing a role in a social process with him.

Types of construct

The fundamental postulate and its corollaries formally define construct theory, but in addition, Kelly provided a systematic language to describe construing processes. He classified constructs, according to the nature of their control over their elements, into *pre-emptive, constellatory* and *propositional*.

A pre-emptive construct is a construct which pre-empts its elements for membership in its own realm exclusively. This is in effect saying that if this man is a homosexual he is *nothing but* a homosexual. This is a gross restricting of the elaborative possibilities of construing. Whether we meet it in psychotherapy, politics or embedded in our own way of viewing some aspect of our environment, it is essentially a denial of the right of other people and ourselves to re-view, re-interpret and see in a fresh light some part of the world around us.

A *constellatory* construct is a construct which fixes the other realm membership of its elements. This is essentially stereotyped or typological thinking and says in effect that if this man is a *homosexual* then he must be *effeminate, artistic, degenerate* and a *menace to society*. Again it reduces our chances of elaborating or re-viewing our outlook – it is a kind of intellectual package deal.

Finally, Kelly talked of *propositional* constructs, which are those constructs which carry no implications regarding the other realm membership of their elements. These are 'as if' constructs where we are prepared to recognize that we can look upon person X *as a homosexual* and thereby make sense out of a lot of what he says and does. But we are recognizing that this is only *one* way of viewing him and is not some final, absolute or all-comprehending truth. We can equally regard him *as a friend* or *as a chess player* or *as a confused man*. The more propositional our constructs the richer becomes our world and the less likely we are to become irretrievably trapped into a conflict which arises out of the rigidity of our viewpoint.

Be it noted that this last paragraph has been written in a somewhat 'pre-emptive' manner in that reference is repeatedly made to constructs as *being* this or that, when clearly what is being talked about is the capacity of a person to use his constructs in a pre-emptive, propositional or constellatory *mode*.

General diagnostic constructs

Construct theory makes psychology essentially constructions about constructions, it makes it a meta-science, a way of making sense out of the ways in which men make sense of their world. Thus, it carries a number of constructs about construing and these include such ideas as *dilation* versus *constriction*. This refers to a dimension in terms of which we can see a person as either broadening his view of the world in order to reorganize it on a more comprehensive level, or constricting his view in order to minimize apparent incompatibilities.

It is important to remember here that such dimensions as this do not have 'healthy' and 'unhealthy' ends. They are not to be confused with the constructs of the logician who is busily sorting out 'good' from 'bad' thinking. A person can dilate successfully and become a larger personality or extend out into chaos, while another person may constrict and thereby make more tidy and controllable his world, or move inexorably towards the ultimate constriction of suicide.

Another important construct of this type is the idea of *tight* versus *loose* construing. Kelly defines a tight construct as one which leads to unvarying predictions, whereas a loose construct is one which leads to varying predictions but which nevertheless can be identified as a continuing interpretation. (Most technical discriminations are tight constructs, e.g. *electrical* versus *diesel,* whereas many evaluative constructs appear loose, e.g. *beautiful* versus *ugly.* The power output of a diesel engine can be accurately predicted, whereas the fate of an ugly man may be anybody's guess.)

Tightening and loosening is a process whereby we can elaborate our construct systems and deal with the kaleidoscope of events that confront us; it is not any kind of choice between a right and a wrong way of doing things. The failure of psychologists to develop their own discipline by alternating between tight and loose construing is discussed by Bannister in the following terms:

It is one of the most marked and disastrous characteristics of current psychology that there has been a cleavage into loose and tight *types of psychology.* This is to say many psychologists seem to fail to move repeatedly through the cycle but rather take up a permanent intellectual residence at one or other end of the cycle.

Thus, we have almost totally loose circumspective psychologies such as Freudian or Existential psychology. This is the kind of speculative, vague psychologizing which leads to papers of the *Unconscious aggression and overt sexual fantasies as quasi-religious substrata for international conflicts* type. At the other end of the spectrum we have the tight world of the pure learning theorist dealing in the highly defined and fragmentary and providing us with the *Short term memory for T mazes under electrically induced stress conditions in the decorticate woodlouse* type of paper. Thus, psychologists tend to take up residence and spend their lives with either the vaguely significant or the specifically irrelevant rather than accept that it is a continuous movement between loose and tight construing that enables the arguments which constitute a science to be elaborated. This kind of frozen positioning seems to underlie much of the tough minded *versus* tender minded argument in science and is obviously referred to by phrases concerning the problem of vitality of material *versus* precision of method (Bannister, 1970, p. 59).

Where did emotion go to?

A common charge levelled against personal construct theory, even by those who admire it (e.g. Bruner, 1956), is that it is too 'mentalistic'.

It is felt that the description of construct systems is purely a description of 'thinking' and thereby deals with only one aspect of man, 'rational' man. But Kelly did not accept the cognition–emotion division as intrinsically valid. It is a jargon descendant of the ancient dualities of *reason* versus *passion, mind* versus *body, flesh* versus *spirit* which has led to dualist psychologies. Construct theory is an attempt to talk about man in a unitary language. We must not misunderstand the theory and assume that a construct is simply words. Because the theory itself is systematic, articulate and rational, it is not claiming that man is systematic, articulate and rational. We may find that we can do much more without the cognition–emotion distinction than we have been able to do with it. Kelly seeks to deal with the kind of problems which are, in both common sense psychology and most modern psychology, dealt with in terms of the concept of 'emotion' or 'drive' or 'motivation', but he tries to remain within the general framework of his own theory and not have recourse to extraneous concepts. 'Emotion' is an hydraulic concept, a vision of some kind of ginger pop fizzing about the human system and it sets up a kind of dichotomy in psychological theory which makes for very great problems.

In order to avoid this dualism Kelly focuses our attention on certain specific constructs, namely *anxiety, hostility, guilt, threat, fear* and *aggression,* but defines them all as 'awareness' that construct systems are in *transitional* states. His specific definitions are as follows.

1. Anxiety is the awareness that the events with which a man is confronted lie mostly outside the range of convenience of his construct system.

We become anxious when we can only partially construe the events which we encounter and too many of their implications are obscure. Sex for the chaste, adulthood for the adolescent, books for the illiterate, power for the humble and death for nearly all of us tend to provoke anxiety. It is the *unknown* aspects of things that go bump in the night that give them their potency. This definition is reasonably specific but it does not involve us in thinking of anxiety as some sort of separate factor inside us. The 'separate factor' theory is implied in common sense statements such as 'He was driven by his anxiety' or psychological statements which talk about a person's 'level of anxiety' as if it were a kind of permanent trait at a given degree of intensity. Moreover, Kelly's is a purely psychological definition of anxiety which does not require us to mix our metaphors further by recourse to physiological constructs.

2. Hostility is the continued effort to extort validational evidence in favour of a type of social prediction which has already been recognized as a failure.

There are times when, if his construct system is to be preserved, a person simply cannot afford to be wrong. If he acknowledges that some of his expectations are ill-founded, this might involve the modification or abandonment of the constructions on which those expectations were based. If in turn, these constructions are central to the whole of his system, he might well be faced with chaos, having no alternative way of viewing his situation. In such a position the person is likely to become *hostile,* to extort evidence, to bully people into behaving in ways which confirm his predictions, to cook the books, to refuse to recognize the ultimate significance of what is happening.

Hostility may appear in many forms, ranging from the mistreatment of neighbours to the point where they counter-attack and provide 'proof' of a cherished theory that people are untrustworthy, to a simple denial of the validity of *the source* of evidence which is too crucially disconfirming. It can take the form of the overt paranoid delusion which uses a 'conspiracy' theory so that all evidence is controvertible. A person may cease to be hostile only when he can find alternative ways of interpreting himself and his situation, that is to say, find some way of making sense of it rather than plunge into chaos. Hostility is defined in terms of its self-preserving function for the individual who is hostile, rather than in terms of a largely unexplained, antagonistic emotion.

3. Guilt is the awareness of dislodgement of the self from one's core role structure.

The term core role structure refers to the system of constructs which deals specifically with the self. They are the dimensions in terms of which a person evaluates the central aspects of his own behaviour, the personal issues with which he is most concerned, the ways in which he tries to anticipate his own future directions and activities. Thus, if you find yourself doing, in important respects, those things you would not have expected to do if you are the kind of person you always thought you were, then you suffer from guilt. Note that the level of abstraction of this definition of guilt is high enough to free us from any need to refer to particular moral codes or cultural standards of behaviour. A person may feel guilty because he finds himself doing those things which other individuals or social reference groups might well consider 'good' things to do. To live in a world where you cannot understand and predict others can be terrifying – how much more terrifying is it to find that one cannot understand or predict oneself. It is, therefore, not surprising that the awareness that we are about to become a mystery to ourselves may produce the kind of ritualistic and rule-ridden behaviour (hostile behaviour in Kelly's sense of the term) which is typical of those who are experiencing guilt.

4. Threat is the awareness of an imminent comprehensive change in one's core structures.

Just as we have a particular core group of constructs in terms of which we try to understand ourselves (core role structure) so we have constructs which subsume the most important aspects of the external world for us and which can be invalidated so as to produce the feeling of threat. We are threatened when our major beliefs about the nature of our personal, social and practical situation are invalidated and the world around us appears about to become chaotic. Threat is an extremely important construct for anyone engaged in attempts to help other people. For example, the psychotherapist in his enthusiasm to change what he considers to be the restrictive and poorly developed ideas of his client may plunge the client into over-hasty experimentation and thereby threaten him. The client may then either become hostile and resist all change or may plunge into the kind of chaos that earns him the title of psychotic. By threatening, in the construct theory sense of the term, we do psychological violence to a person.

5. Fear is the awareness of an imminent incidental change in one's core structures.

When only a more peripheral part of our world becomes meaningless and unpredictable, we experience fear. Our superordinate constructions are not invalidated, so we have no sense of being overwhelmed, but an area of darkness opens up before us and however circumscribed it might be, we feel fear at the impending change.

6. Aggression is the active elaboration of one's perceptual field.

It is interesting to note that Kelly is here attempting to define aggression (and similarly attempts to define hostility) in terms of what is going on *within the individual* rather than in terms of other people's reaction to him. Thus, a person is being aggressive when he actively experiments to check the validity of his construing; when he extends the range of his constructions (and thereby his activities) in new directions; when he is exploring. Obviously from the point of view of the people around and about such a person, this can be a very uncomfortable process and they may well see it as an attack upon them and handle it as such. But in terms of the aggressive person's construction system it is essentially an extending and elaborating process and thereby the opposite of hostility.

Just as there is no onus on Kelly (or any other theorist) to build a general concept of 'emotion' into his theory, he is not obliged to provide exact equivalents for particular 'emotions'. However, his theory can be required to provide explanations for the kinds of problem-phenomena which are dealt with under the rubric of this or that 'emotion'. Consider, for example, the kind of commitment which, in lay psychological theories, is dealt with under the concept of 'being in love'. From a construct theory viewpoint we might look on love as a form of role relationship, not in the sense that the two people concerned are acting out socially prescribed parts, but in the sense that they are aggressively elaborating themselves, their construct systems – core role structures – by experimenting with their understanding of each other. 'Being in love' is probably the situation in which most of us experience the greatest possibility of really elaborating ourselves and thereby take our greatest personal risk. Each, in living out the relationship, is putting to the test his implicit interpretation of the nature of the other and thereby extending his understanding of himself since we use another's reaction to us (filtered through our interpretation of them) in developing a picture of ourselves. However, since core role constructs are central to 'being in love' then much is at risk. If our core construing is validated, we may elaborate and become truly a larger person – if we are invalidated then we may need to become hostile, in Kelly's sense of the term, in order to avert chaos. We may then break up the relationship in order to deny the authenticity of the other person as a source of evidence. Alternatively a love affair could be developed on a hostile basis in that the partners might bully each other into providing supporting evidence for a crumbling theory of themselves. The essence of the relationship is then that no genuine risk is taken, no falsifiable hypothesis is ventured, the books are cooked, the experiment rigged, the evidence worthless, because the witnesses have bribed each other.

A commentary on love in these terms may seem inappropriate because it is 'rational' and love is said to be 'irrational', but such a view confuses event with interpretation. Kelly (1966b) argues as follows:

The man in love may see nothing rational in his experience and he may go so far as to regard himself as the unwitting victim of psychodynamics or love potions. But that does not mean that we must limit ourselves to the same terms he uses. Our job is to understand his experience in general, not merely to simulate it in particular. To do this with any perspicacity we must devise our own constructions. Our constructs must enable us to subsume his constructs, not simulate them merely. If he thinks in terms of psychodynamics, that is something we ought to understand and appreciate. But it is not necessary for us to resort to psychodynamic explanations ourselves in order to understand his construct of 'psychodynamics'.

Stressing the redefinition of 'emotion' into terms which have to do with transition, process and change, Kelly developed the idea of the circumspection–pre-emption–control cycle (CPC cycle). This is the sequence of construction involving, in succession, circumspection, pre-emption and control, which leads to choice. Kelly is here emphasizing the way in which construct systems move and flow. Initially we circumspect the field (dream, imagine, speculate), trying to achieve pre-emption. At this point we begin to select out certain issues as crucial and decide what kind of situation we are in. Finally we move to control, the point at which we make active choices which are to be elaborated. We decide not only what construct will cover the situation, but which pole of that construct will give us the best anticipatory base for action.

These constructs about transition all seem, in some

measure, to relate to the traditional definitions of terms such as anxiety, guilt and so forth. But they are defined so as to be part of a unitary theory and so avoid the dualistic notion that inside each of us there are two men, a 'reasoning' man and a 'feeling' man, these being unrelated except that each hinders and obstructs the progress of the other. For Kelly, such a dualism is a badly articulated attempt to cope with the fact that man is a process and that at different stages in the process very different modes of experience and activity obtain.

The terms and formal aspects of construct theory are given in full as an appendix, but it is essential in evaluating them to bear in mind what is meant by the central idea of a construct. A construct, it must be repeated, is not a verbal label. Constructs can be pre-verbal (were developed before the child had a labelling system available to him), they can have partial verbal labels as when the one pole is named, but there is no verbal tag whereby one can recognize the opposite pole. A person may have verbal labels for constructs at one level but be unaware of the lines of relationship and implications between different parts of his construct network. This provides him with a kind of 'unconscious'; endowing him with both resources and problems that he cannot readily put into words. A construct is essentially a discrimination which the person can make. Construct theory is an attempt to understand people in terms of the way each experiences the world and to understand their behaviour in terms of what it is designed to signify for the behaving person.

Kelly (1966b) defines construing, in the following passage, as man's attempt to transcend the obvious.

To transcend the obvious – this is the basic problem of man. Inevitably it is a problem we must all seek to solve, whether we fancy ourselves as psychologists or not. What has already happened in our experience may seem obvious enough, now that we have been through it. But literally it is something that will never happen again. It can't, for time refuses to run around in circles. If then, as we live our lives, we do no more than erect a row of historical markers on the spots where we have had our experiences, we shall soon find ourselves surrounded by a cemetery of monuments, and overburdened with biographical mementoes.

But to represent an event by means of a construct is to go beyond what is known. It is to see that event in a way that could possibly happen again. Thus, being human and capable of construing, we can do more than point realistically to what has happened in the past; we can actually set the stage for what may happen in the future – something, perhaps in some respects, very different. Thus we transcend the obvious! By construing we reach beyond anything that man has heretofore known – often reach in vain, to be sure, but sometimes with remarkable prescience. This paper has to do with how man, from his position of relative ignorance, can hope to reach out for knowledge that no one has yet attained. This, as I see it, is a primary problem for the psychologist, though I doubt that most psychologists see it that way.

Psychology and values

A theoretical framework in psychology – unlike theoretical frameworks in the natural sciences – inevitably proposes values. Incantatory insistence on being purely 'objective' does not enable us to escape the moral issues which are implicit in psychology. The declared aims of science – prediction and control – have moral connotations immediately we realize that it is human beings that we are proposing to predict and control. A psychological theory is inevitably not only a statement about people, it is an attitude towards them, a way of relating to them. The view of man as a mechanism, implicit in learning theory, can naturally be extended to support a manipulative attitude towards men. The Freudian portrait of man as essentially infantile, trapped in his own inadequate attempts to deal with his sexual, aggressive, destructive and death-seeking drives is also an evaluation of man. It places the psychoanalysed psychoanalyst in the position of priest to penitent where other men are concerned. Construct theory can be seen as evaluating man and proposing a relationship between so-called psychologist and so-called subject in the following terms (Bannister, 1970b):

Construct theory sees each man as trying to make sense out of himself and his world. It sees psychology as a meta-discipline, an attempt to make sense out of the ways in which men make sense out of their worlds. This not only puts the psychologist in the same interpretive business as his so-called subject – it makes them partners in the business, for on no other basis can one man understand another, however many successful short-term predictions he may make or successful short-term behavioural modifications he may assay.

The distinction between individual man and social man is well lost in construct theory. The theory proposes that our picture of our own individuality is built up by our assessment of others' pictures of us. Not that we simply accept the evaluations of others but we use them as evidence, weighed against our construing of their construction processes. This makes the individual never less than self-identified by never more than he can understand of others.

The moral of this tale is not that, in order to be psychologists, we must abandon science and rest content with personal rules of thumb, the insights of the artist, the verities of legend or the perspectives of history. It is rather that our theories should not gainsay – though they need not simply describe and may extend – our personal experience. They should involve us in, rather than detach us from, our subject-matter. In terms of the argument of this paper, they should betoken a relationship with man that would liberate and challenge him rather than diminish him.

It is true that construct theory is an optimistic theory in the sense that it can envisage optimal man as well as minimal man and in the sense that it proposes itself as an elaborative tool which men might use to extend their own possibilities. However, it enables us to offer explanations for man at his most vicious as well as at his most aspiring. Men do truly follow their constructions to the point where, if they construe other men as being something substantially less than human, they are thereby enabled to torment and destroy them. Thus the family-loving concentration camp guard is enabled to go cheerfully about his diabolical business.

In the following chapters examples will be given of how aspects of the theory have been or might be used in an effort to understand the person. Wherever there is repetition this is not for its own sake, but rather it underlines the contention of construct theory that man is a totality and cannot readily be segmented into category headings for the convenience of authors.

There have been a number of attempts to summarize personal construct theory and examine its relationship to 'mainstream' psychology – these include Bannister (1962b), Sechrest (1963), Bonarius (1965), Bannister and Mair (1968), Geiwitz (1969) and Pervin (1970). Obviously the ultimate value and fate of the theory will be decided by how useful people find it as experimental psychologists, as therapists, as individuals, but it is clear that its visible scope and implication merit inspection and testing.

2 The Person in Psychology

Speech is not what one should desire to understand. One should know the speaker. . . . The deed is not what one should desire to understand. One should know the doer. . . . Mind is not what one should desire to understand. One should know the thinker.

KANSHITAKI, *Upanishad*, iii, 8

A theory of *personal* constructs argues that the person is the irreducible unit in psychology. The fundamental postulate of the theory reads: 'A *person's* processes are psychologically channellized by the ways in which he anticipates events.' Kelly (1955) goes on to say: 'This term (person) is used to indicate the substance with which we are primarily concerned. Our first consideration is the individual person rather than any part of the person, any group of persons, or any particular processes manifested in the person's behaviour.' To emphasize this point further, ten out of the eleven elaborative corollaries of the theory make specific reference to the 'person'.

Modern psychology is not, in the main, about persons, and so by making the person the central subject matter of psychology, construct theory changes the boundaries and the content of the science. However, before we consider what psychology has been about (while it was not being about persons), let us attempt a brief definition of *the person*. Let us begin, not by looking outside at other people to see whether we are going to allow them the dignity of being persons, but by deriving an initial definition from looking inside at ourselves.

It is argued that *you* consider *yourself* a person in that:

1. You entertain a notion of your own separateness from others, you rely on the privacy of your own consciousness.

2. You entertain a notion of the integrity and completeness of your own experience, so that you believe all parts of it are relatable because you are the experiencer.

3. You entertain a notion of your own continuity over time, you possess your own biography and live in relation to it.

4. You entertain a notion of the causality of your actions, you have purposes, you intend, you accept a partial responsibility for the effects of what you do.

5. You entertain a notion of other persons by analogy with yourself, you assume a comparability of subjective experience.

In summary, you see yourself as *self-inventing*.

Obviously, in our role as psychologists we *can* reject the concept of a person by analogy with ourselves. We *can* (and many psychologists do) try to look upon other persons as moving objects, explicable in mechanical terms. From a construct theory point of view it is argued that we will understand, explain and predict more about people, particularly over the course of time, if we centre our thinking on the idea of a person. This is quite apart from the argument that it would be an act of grace so to do. It can be argued that much of traditional psychology has achieved a rather miserable and inadequate statement of its subject because it has declined to use the idea of a person. What then have psychologists studied instead of studying the person?

Behaviour

Psychologists have studied 'behaviour'.

The reverence with which 'behaviour' is spoken of in psychology probably stems from the half-expressed conviction that behaviour alone is 'real' and psychology itself is a mass of 'concepts' so that unless we cling steadfastly to behaviour the whole business may turn out to be a ghastly, ghostly and above all unscientific misadventure.

The philosophical assumptions of construct theory are explicit and they include an acceptance of a reality 'out there'; it is not a solipsistic theory. But it does argue that we cannot know reality directly. We can only construe and interpret it, usefully or uselessly. The same is true of the reality we call 'behaviour'. Immediately we label it, assess it, or even select it by pointing to it, we have placed a construction upon it. The instant we begin to talk of a twitching toe we are already deep into the semantics of the construct system which defines 'twitching' and defines 'toe' and which separates them out as entities. If we see a man walking along the street, we may say that he is 'going to the cinema' or 'manifesting motor movement' or 'dawdling' or 'manifesting adient rather than abient behaviour', but whatever we say of it, we shall have construed. We shall not have made some miraculous interpretation-free contact with reality. True, 'behavioural' terms are terms at a low level of abstraction, but they are still terms *at a level of abstraction*. And, of course, concepts such as stimulus, response, reward, punishment, drive, negative and positive reinforcement, are all concepts at an enormously high level of abstraction, certainly at as high a level of abstraction as concepts like 'mind'. They are about as near to behaviour as the construct Neanderthal is to the chipped flint to which it is applied.

Still, it is true that in so far as science requires operational definitions and common sense demands that we get down to brass tacks, any psychological theory will have to wrestle with and predict in terms of behaviour. But instead of trying to treat behaviour in its own right, construct theory argues that behaviour must be related to the person who behaves. What a person does, he does to some purpose and he not only behaves, but he intends to indicate something by his behaviour. Indeed, in construct theory terms, behaviour becomes not a reaction but a proposition, not the answer but the question. As Kelly (1970a) has pointed out, behaviour is an experiment and in behaving a man is asking a question of his world – a man's behaviour will make little ultimate sense to us unless we understand the question which he is asking. Behaviour, like words (referred to by psychologists as verbal behaviour), has *meaning* and changing and elaborating meaning at that.

Comparative psychology

Psychologists have avoided studying man the person by studying man the animal. True, we *can* study 'man the animal' just as we *can* study 'man the organic system' as in physiology. The implication of referring to psychology as a 'biological science' is presumably to argue that man should be seen in perspective as one of the 'higher' animals. From this point of view it makes sense to study the rat, the cat, the pigeon, the octopus, the woodlouse and the cockroach because, in so far as we are seeing man as an elaboration of these, what is discovered of them is at least potentially relevant.

But we are entitled to study man as anything we wish – it is our choice because sciences are invented not discovered. And if we wish to understand man *as a person,* then comparative studies cannot have even indirect relevance. From a construct theory point of view the upside-down anthropomorphism of comparative psychology is properly the domain of the biologist or zoologist. Such studies, however competent or thoughtful, are in a language which renders them irrelevant to the understanding of man as a person.

Presumably, concepts like 'drive' are favoured because they are seen as spanning the distance between man and the animals and including them both within their range of convenience. Such concepts – like the notions it is currently fashionable to import from ethology – have a meagre value as metaphors, but they are not the stuff of a science of psychology.

The futility of the attempt to erect psychological constructs on the basis of biological elements is exemplified by Vince's (1967) study entitled 'Respiration as a factor in communication between quail embryos'. The key point here is the curious use of the term 'communication'. The study showed that the 'clicking' of quail eggs increases in speed as hatching time approaches. The effect within the clutch of quail eggs is that the faster clickers speed up the slower clickers and the slower clickers slow down the faster clickers, the result being that the quail eggs hatch out more or less together. From a utilitarian point of view – in avoiding problems for the mother quail in being faced simultaneously with wandering chicks and incubating eggs – this seems a reasonable arrangement. As a purely zoological study the research is admirable.

However, why the term 'communication'? Avalanches of stones moving down a mountain side presumably work on something like the same basis in that fast stones are slowed down by collision with slow stones and slow stones are speeded up by collision with fast stones, with the net result that the stones tend to arrive at the bottom of the mountain somewhat together. However we do not talk about the stones 'communicating' and we would not be likely to produce a paper called 'Collision as a factor in communication between avalanching stones'. The term 'communication' seems to have very little meaning when applied to the embryo quail beyond that which it would have in the avalanche context. Certainly it can carry none of the meaning that we are entitled to give it in a psychological context. Indeed, when we consider titles for research like 'Social enhancement and impairment of performance in the cockroach' we become aware that we are trying to build psychology on the basis of weak puns. And at the level of 'Some observations of the behaviour of woodlice in a magnetic field' (Johnson, 1969) even the effort at analogy seems to have failed and the presence of such researches in psychological journals is one of the mysteries of modern psychology.

Be it noted that the argument here is not about whether man is an animal or not. Certainly he is an animal, just as he is a collection of chemicals, an organic system and a mass of whirling electrons. The argument is whether it would be more rewarding for all concerned if psychologists studied him 'as an animal' or studied him 'as a person'.

Social psychology

In so far as it has involved a study of interpersonal interaction and used concepts implying a high level of consciousness such as 'attitude', social psychology has contributed to our understanding of man as a person. Indeed, it may be that most of the ideas relevant to a study of the person are at present to be found under the rubric of social psychology. However, psychologists have followed custom in establishing social psychology as a mini-psychology in its own right and have thereby hindered the development of a general psychology of persons. Equally, in making the *group* their focus of convenience, social psychologists have lost much of the meaning of the individual person within the group and the meaning of the group to the individual person.

Consider for example what social psychologists have made of the potentially invaluable idea of 'role' by seeing it too completely in group terms. Kelly (1966a) put it as follows:

Role can be understood in terms of what the person *himself* is doing rather than in terms of his circumstances. There are two traditional notions of role, one the very old notion that role is a course of action which is articulated with the actions of others, so that together you and the other person can produce something. The more recent notion proposed by sociologists and other theorists is that a role is a set of expectations held by others within which a man finds himself encompassed and surrounded. Personal construct theory tries to put role within the context of something a person himself is doing and it springs from a notion that one may attempt to understand others in terms of their outlooks just as a personal construct theory psychologist tries to understand human beings in terms of their outlooks.

So anyone who attempts to understand others in terms of the outlooks they have, rather than their behaviours only, may indeed play a role. This isn't to say that he tries to conform to their outlooks, he may even try to stand them on their heads, but if he tries to understand others by putting on their spectacles and then does something, then that which he does could be considered as a role. So we have three notions of role here. The oldest notion, the notion of a course of activity articulated with the action of others, I suppose that notion could be tied up with the notion of man as the economic entity, 'the economic man'.

The more recent notion of man surrounded by a set of expectations, I suppose you can say would be a notion that would
undergird the society which had seen itself composed of 'ideo-
logical men' conforming to ideas, ideologies. But if we follow the
notion of role that comes out of construct theory, I wonder if we
might not develop the notion of man as a society composed of
'empathic man' or 'inquiring man'. Men who seem to understand
and do it by active inquiry, using their own behaviour not as
something to act out, but as a means of understanding their
world.

Kelly is here pointing to the sociality corollary which says
that 'to the extent that one person construes the construction
processes of another he may play a role in a social process
involving the other person'. This definition relates the 'individual' to the 'social' and makes role more than simply a
socially prescribed dialogue. Indeed the integration of social
and individual or general psychology (their original sep-
aration seems to have been a way of impoverishing both)
might well centre on re-thinking, in construct theory terms,
the idea of role.

Personality

The study of personality would seem to be inescapably the
study of the person and yet again, by demoting it to being a
topic or area *within* psychology, the equivalence of the
terms 'psychological' and 'personal' has been lost. If psychology were truly the study of the person, we would no
longer have 'personality' as a separate topic, any more than
we would have work on 'problem-solving' which did not
include the solving of personal problems, or have 'person
perception' as a special and rather suspect part of the
general study of perception.

The castrating effect of separating personality off as a
mini-psychology in its own right is perhaps best seen in the
curiously named study of 'individual differences', which in
fact turns out to be the study of group samenesses. As a
result we have focused on the establishment of general
dimensions, at some point along which all individuals can

be placed, rather than on a study of the dimensions which each individual develops in order to organize his own world. Mair (1970) comments thus:

Psychologists, of course, repeatedly involve people in their experiments, but relatively few experimenters seem concerned with them as individuals, preferring generally to see each one as part of a fairly anonymous subject pool. So widely accepted is this view that some may not think it very important that there are striking features of individual people as we know them from everyday experience to which 'experimental' or 'scientific' psychology pays little heed. My own belief, however, is that whatever else it may concern itself with, psychology should be concerned centrally with defining and elaborating individual experience and action. In suggesting that psychology should be fundamentally about individuals, I am not proposing an isolationist, anti-social view since I am convinced of the irretrievably interpersonal nature of each person's system for organizing and making sense of himself and the world around him. Neither am I suggesting that groups should be excluded from the study, but wish only to draw attention to the fact that more often than not the study of groups is merely the superficial study of a number of individuals at the same time; the presence of so many people being surreptitiously used as justification for the impersonal and insensitively standardized approach to any particular individual involved.

The attempt to encompass the person within the study of personality is additionally bedevilled by the strange persistence of trait psychology. The habit of seeing others in a rather simple, rigid and typological manner has stunted the life of many individuals and its formalization in psychology has had the same effect upon the discipline. Hartshorne and May (1928) found that their experimental subjects were not consistently 'honest' or 'dishonest' and the argument as to whether individuals have consistent characteristics still goes on. But the question being asked by psychologists is still 'does the individual's behaviour appear consistent *in my terms*?' A more rewarding question might be 'is the individual's behaviour consistent *in his own terms*?' The psychologist's task is then to understand those terms and relate behaviour to them.

Segmented man

Long ago the old and apparently discredited 'faculties' of faculty psychology won their final victory when they were transmuted and came to make up the entire field by each attaining the status of a mini-psychology in its own right. The standard chapter headings of memory, cognition, motivation, perception, emotion, the senses and so forth are the ultimate denial of the person as the subject matter of psychology. They substitute for the person functions to be studied separately, in spite of the fact that they cannot be *lived* separately. Any experimental psychologist who has ever done a study of, say, memory, has watched his stubborn subjects continue to cognize, emote, perceive, sense and so on, even though the experiment called upon them only to remember.

Consider the study of 'memory' as an area. It began with the work of Ebbinghaus who sought scientific purity by using nonsense syllables as his material to be remembered. But man *as a person* does not choose to remember nonsense, though man *as an experimental subject* might. Nearly fifty years later Bartlett (1932) clearly argued that memory be placed back in the context of the person (note he uses 'we' in the final paragraph of his classic work):

I have written a book preoccupied 'in the main', with problems of remembering and its individual and social determination. But I have never regarded memory as a faculty, as a reaction narrowed and ringed around, containing all its peculiarities and all their explanations within itself. I have regarded it rather as one achievement in the line of the ceaseless struggle to master and enjoy a world full of variety and rapid change. Memory, and all the life of images and words which goes with it, is one with the age-old acquisition of the distance senses, and with that development of constructive imagination and constructive thought wherein at length we find the most complete release from the narrowness of present time and place (Bartlett, 1932, p. 314).

Nearly fifty years after this contention we are still witnessing the continuation of an arid stream of 'memory' experiments, 'bowing' and 'chunking' the serial learning curve apparently for evermore. Deese (1969) summarizes the position thus:

Despite the existence of an embarrassingly large number of experiments in which rote learning of some materials has been controlled and varied in time of exposure or trials, we still do not know whether there is some link between number of exposures and how well people learn (a condition we cannot even characterize adequately in behavioural terms, so we resort to the quagmire of concepts centering around response strength and associative strength). That the experimental psychology of rote learning has been unable to solve so simple and elementary a problem should lead us to question whether or not we are going about things in the right way. Certainly, almost anyone but an experimental psychologist would long ago have begun to entertain doubts.

It seems likely that the attraction of 'segmented man' and the chapter heading approach to psychology lies in the freedom from the discipline of theory which such an approach offers. The intellectual carve-up encourages the kind of empirical approach marked by cafeteria thinking. The psychologist arbitrarily defines his problem in convenient and empirical terms and selects, on a cafeteria basis, whatever concepts suit his immediate purpose. He then solves the problem in terms as arbitrary and *ad hoc* as those in which it was originally posed. This kind of procedure has some short-term applied pay-offs, but it is an effective way of inhibiting the growth of a science.

Physiological psychology

Physiological psychology represents a complete evasion of the person as an issue in psychology, since the person is no more his cerebral cortex than he is his left earhole (cf. Bannister, 1968).

Perhaps the fascination which neurophysiological concepts have for many psychologists stems from their yearning to have direct contact with and 'know' reality, rather than understand that it can only be construed. In some strange way, it seems to be thought that because the concepts of physiological psychology refer to tiny 'units beneath the skin', we have here the kind of 'reality' that the physicist is assumed to have when he talks of atoms and molecules. Bannister argued:

Perhaps the key to misconceptions in this type of reductionism is the notion that problems (or phenomena or areas of study) exist somehow independently of the sciences which define them. A chemical 'problem' is one which is stated *in chemical terms* and a psychological problem is so because it represents alternative lines of implication for a group of *psychological* concepts (this is why it is a problem). As such it cannot be solved in non-psychological terms. What may happen is that some other problem involving similar operational definitions is set up in other (e.g. neurophysiological) terms. This can be solved in such neurophysiological terms but the psychologically defined problem has not thereby been 'transcended' or 'reduced', it remains to be solved in its own terms (Bannister, 1970c, p. 415).

Thus, when psychologists study brain damage they attempt to mimic the physiologist who is sensibly committed in his own terms to studying man *as an organic system*, not *as a person*. The psychologist studies how damage to the brain causes defects which can be construed in mechanical terms, e.g. shuffling, slurring of speech, paralysis. At best he uses a fractional-functional model as in studies of memory failure. It is significant that he does not study what the 'brain damaged' person makes of himself *as a person* living with these handicaps. Does he remake his ideals from those of Napoleon to those of St Francis? How does he see his limitations? These and related questions are validly *psychological*. The currently popular questions are properly the outer boundaries of neurophysiology.

The outlawed person

This discourse on the *ways* in which psychologists (intentionally or unintentionally) have excluded the person from their field of study still leaves us with the question of why they have done this. Two considerations may have inspired their continual detour around the person.

Firstly, making the person the centre of study might well preclude them from playing 'the science game' as it is now understood. We would have to re-imagine our experiments instead of concretistically mimicking the procedures of the chemist or the physicist. This, because persons (as distinct from functions or behaviours or physiological readings or rats) are potentially as much experimenters as we are. Thus, the traditional 'experimenter-subject' roles would have to be abandoned. We could, for example, review our picture of the behaviour therapist as he 'shapes' the mute schizophrenic's speech by making gifts of sweets or cigarettes contingent upon the production of speech. We might have to recognize the validity of the mute schizophrenic as a person who is 'shaping' the psychologist's behaviour by making the gift of speech contingent upon sweet or cigarette-giving.

Secondly, so long as we continue to exclude the person from the discourse of psychology, then we can continue to ignore the relationship between our professional and personal lives. Mair has pointed out:

The dilemma facing psychologists who wish to acknowedge the specifically human features of those they study (rather than the features men share with animals) is a dilemma just because psychologists too are human. When they recognize that their subjects share many of the concerns and capacities of experimenters, they must also appreciate that they, as experimenters, share the limitations of ordinary people. Psychologists, like other people, have to work within the bounds set by their own achievements and hope to extend their competence only through the means they are capable of employing. Each has a limited viewpoint, personal and often unacknowledged assumptions, preferred theories and explanations, favoured methods for raising and answering questions. Like others, a psychologist can only subsume the assumptions, theories, methods and actions of others in relation to his personal points of view and to the extent that his own sense-making system allows (Mair, 1970b, p. 182).

Recognition that psychology is a science of persons invented by persons would involve us in making our personal values explicit in relation to professional issues. Currently personal values guide our professional lives – as inevitably they must – but are not avowed.

Clearly, a re-focusing of psychology on to the person does not mean a simple rejection of all that has gone before. Much of it can be reinterpreted to throw light on our understanding of persons, although, since psychology is an invention and not a discovery, we are under no obligation to carry forward everything that has ever been done in its name. It would be to our advantage to leave much behind. Such a re-focusing of psychology on to the person would make the work of psychologists much more interrelatable, so that viewpoints, methods, theories and hypotheses would often be competitive. In the past, the carving up of the field into mini-psychologies has allowed a 'live and let live' policy. Each psychologist has been free to stake his own claim and produce work which had no implications, nice or nasty, for the endeavours of those in other territories. This disintegrated but comfortable mode of developing the discipline might come to an abrupt end.

This then is the central feature of personal construct theory. It is not a theory *within* psychology as at present practised, but it is a proposal that the focus and boundaries of the discipline be redefined and it thereby explicitly challenges the very shape of traditional psychology.

3 Assessment of the Person

The first thing the intellect does with an object is to class it along with something else. But any object that is infinitely important to us and awakens our devotion feels to us also as if it must be *sui generis* and unique. Probably a crab would be filled with a sense of personal outrage if it could hear us class it without ado or apology as a crustacean, and thus dispose of it. 'I am no such thing,' it would say: '*I am myself, myself alone.*'

WILLIAM JAMES
The Varieties of Religious Experience:
A Study in Human Nature
Gifford Lectures, 1901–2

The way we look at things determines what we *do* about measuring or changing those things; be it the problem child at school, racial prejudice, disturbed behaviour in the individual, or such whirlpool concepts as 'personality'. Traditionally, psychologists have worked within category distinctions about the aspects of man to be studied – he learns (learning), perceives (perception), thinks (cognition), has drives (motivation) and so forth. The 'person', as such, has been rarely and obliquely dealt with under such headings as 'person perception' or by equating the person with his 'reinforcement history' or by regarding him as a source of error variance encountered when trying to measure generalities.

Theory or catch-as-catch-can

While there are coherent theoretical frameworks for the psychologist to employ, there are many who mix parts of unrelated theories to account for man's behaviour. Harsh things have been written about such eclecticism. Boring (1950) speaks of 'sheer eclectic laziness' and (1929) refers to the 'eclectically-minded, middle-of-the-road nonentity'. In his paper entitled 'The fruits of eclecticism – bitter or sweet?', Allport (1964) defines eclecticism as 'a system that seeks the solution of fundamental problems by selecting and uniting what it regards as true in the several specialized approaches to psychological science'. He points out the great difficulty, if not the impossibility, of the task the eclectic sets himself. He has somehow to integrate a great diversity of results from very different levels of discourse.

One of the great illusions in psychology is that 'facts' can be added together and that, come the day of Jubilo, they will be united under one theoretical framework. Only if one works within a theory can an integrated sequence of hypotheses be derived and the experimental findings systematically added to our knowledge. Pure 'fact' gathering is, in any case, a myth. The very selection of this rather than that 'fact' as relevant to our understanding implies assumptions which constitute the psychologist's hidden, unformulated and probably internally contradictory theory.

The individual as a universe of discourse

Kelly's emphasis on the study of the individual person highlights a readiness for re-focusing in psychology which has been growing over the past twenty years. Particularly significant is the increasing realization that it is possible to study the data from one individual person (idiography) as well as data from a number of individuals (nomothesis). As long ago as 1955, Du Mas outlined rules for analysing data from one person.

Opinion as to the place of these two approaches in a scientific discipline range from that of Bills (1938), who viewed psychology as a wholly nomothetic discipline, to William James (1891) who defined psychology as 'the science of finite minds'. It is, and indeed has been for many a year, the dominant fashion to use nomothetic methods, but an in-

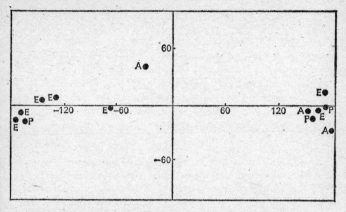

Figure 1 Map of semantic differential scales representing three
factors: Evaluative (E), Activity (A) and Potency (P)
(From Fransella, 1965)

creasing number of psychologists express dissatisfaction
with the results obtained and the generalizations that can be
made about individuals. Their disquiet rests upon demon-
strations that only under very special circumstances do
'averaged curves' have the same form as any of the 'individual' curves from which they are derived. One can seldom
draw meaningful inferences about individual processes from
group statistics (e.g. Sidman, 1952; Bakan, 1954).

Figure 1 shows how the three nomothetic dimensions of
meaning in a 'semantic differential' are not identifiable when
analysed for one person instead of a group. The semantic
differential (Osgood *et al.*, 1957) was a very ambitious attempt
to establish general psychological dimensions of word meaning which would hold good for all men in all places. Theoretically, the *activity* words (A's) in Figure 1 should cluster
together and be in a different part of the 'semantic space'
from all *evaluative* words (E's), and all *potency* words (P's)
should be separated in turn from the other two clusters – but
this is patently not so.

It is interesting to note the steady retreat of semantic differential users from the original stand on the three 'universal' dimensions of *evaluation, activity* and *potency*. For example, Warr and his co-workers (1969) now say 'knowledge of only the average tells us nothing about the dimensions which underlie judgements by a particular individual'.

Having demonstrated this point by plotting differences between subjects' individual learning curves and the grouped curve, Baloff and Becker (1967) point out that Tryon was making exactly this point in 1934 when he said that:

the intensive study of the average behaviour of a species ... generally leads the ... psychologist to ignore the more interesting differences between individuals from whom the 'average individual' is abstracted. The 'average' individual is, in fact, a man-made fiction, and the behaviour of a species can be properly understood only by considering variations in behaviour of all (or a random sample) of the individuals who are classed in it.

The doctrine of norms

The commonality corollary states that we come to share certain constructs if we live in a similar culture, though all the *implications* of these constructs may not be identical – for construct systems are indeed *personal*. In a warrior culture, men do not necessarily agree as to the precise braveness or cowardliness of a particular act, but they do agree that the important aspect of that act is its braveness-cowardliness content. To another culture that reveres logical thinking, whether the person acts in a brave or cowardly way is relatively unimportant; the act of the individual is construed in terms of its logic.

'Culture' specifies the superordinate dimensions along which the acts of individuals are primarily to be construed. It dictates the 'ideal' personality characteristics. Not so long ago, in certain sections of European society 'personal honour' was valued above all else and countless people died in its defence.

Cultural norms, against which the actions of men in a particular group are compared, have considerable relevance to many aspects of life. They underlie psychiatric diagnosis.

A person may deviate from a group standard just so much before being pronounced 'mentally ill' (if he is held to be suffering from some condition over which he has insufficient control); 'criminal', if he is held responsible for his behaviour; 'delinquent', if he is young but responsible; or 'psychoneurotic', if he is not mentally ill but still suffering from such an 'abnormality' of personality that he is not held to be *totally* responsible. There are people about whom society cannot make up its mind. These 'mentally abnormal offenders' (Rollin, 1969) are seen to be mentally ill but sometimes also deemed to be responsible for their acts and so sent to prison when they commit an offence.

There are degrees of deviation as well. If a person is a 'little' mentally ill, he is still likely to be on the 'normal' continuum and so be described as 'neurotic'. But if his behaviour is beyond the cultural pale, he will be labelled 'psychotic'. The study of these deviators then begins. Norms are established for neurotics, norms for delinquents, norms for psychotics, norms for psychopaths and so forth. Only extreme cases will be identifiable in terms of these normative categories. All that can be said normatively of most of us is that we are neither giants nor dwarfs.

There has been a suggestion (Ross 1963) that people who do not conform to the norm (e.g. do not reach a learning criterion in a learning experiment) should be investigated because they are of obvious interest. Presumably, they will make us widen our concepts of deviation. This means that there will be more norms to be added for each new deviant group. Followed to its illogical conclusion, there will be norms for deviant deviants and so on until all research will be on the individual, who then can only deviate from his own 'normative' behaviour.

Personality

Apart from being able to learn, to be motivated, and to think, man has 'personality'. This ragbag category of concepts includes almost every idea about man that has ever been suggested. Since what we measure is specified by our concept of what personality is, it is not surprising that psychologists split into a multitude of factions where the measurement of personality is concerned. In 1937, Allport listed fifty meanings of personality and it is anybody's guess how many there are in 1971. Hall and Lindzey (1957) say they are convinced that '... no substantive definition of personality can be applied with any generality ... we submit that personality is defined by the particular empirical concepts which are a part of the theory of personality employed by the observer.' You pays your money and you takes your pick.

Kelly seems never to have made explicit his definition of the term 'personality', but he repeatedly implies that it is man's way of construing and experimenting with his world. He sets out what he calls 'design specifications for a psychological theory of personality'. In the first place, he considers the perspective should be broad even though the person should be theorizing about *something*. That is, a theory should have a *focus* as well as a *range* of convenience. For him, the focus of convenience of construct theory is the psychotherapeutic encounter; just as for psychoanalytic theory the focus is the psycho-dynamics of the neurotic individual and its range extends to interpretations of the arts and religion. Some theories have a very limited range of convenience, for example, Hull's theory of learning which broke down when attempts were made to extend it to cover personality.

The second design specification is that a theory should be fertile in creating new ideas: 'It should lead to the formulation of hypotheses; it should provoke experiments; and it should inspire invention'. Time will show whether construct theory complies with this specification, but those at present working within its framework believe that it does. In addition, the hypotheses generated should be testable and the theory should eventually be proved valid in that more of its hypotheses are supported by results than are negated. Kelly is of the opinion that a good psychological theory does not have to contain its own operational definitions but it should be capable of generating hypotheses that 'lead to research with operationally defined variables'. A theory should also be capable of extension yet must ultimately prove to be redundant, giving way to a theory that is better able to explain the existing observations and lead to more precise hypotheses. In this way a body of scientific knowledge develops.

Intelligence

A category in terms of which most people are judged at one time or another in their lives is that labelled 'intelligence'. When Binet pioneered his test, it had a specific purpose – to identify those children in France who needed special attention at school to help bring them up to the level of others. Since then psychologists have broadened the construct to include adults and been highly industrious in trying to establish theoretical and operational definitions – failing dismally for the most part. Kelly argues that the notion of IQ has failed to be of general use to adults, not because it could not be measured, nor because it failed to correlate with certain other adult behaviours, but because it did not help very much in increasing our understanding of what people 'could do about themselves and about each other'. Intelligence has been regarded as a trait; we have studied such static and allegedly immutable characteristics when we should have been investigating the *process* of 'thinking', of solving problems, of construing.

Some of the problems about the notion of intelligence are that it has been shown to vary, during childhood particularly; there are cultural differences in the measuring of intelligence and intelligence testing (for example, Bernstein, 1961 and Vernon, 1969); and the testing situation can be altered psychologically by the expectations of both tester (Rosenthal, 1967) and testee (for example, Hudson, 1970). A person's view of himself and society's view of him can profoundly affect performance. An adult or child who considers he is not much good may well not 'try' hard on a test which he knows is to measure the thing he knows he 'lacks'.

Probably the clearest example of this is the finding that

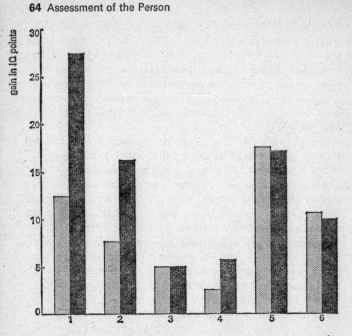

Figure 2 Gains in intelligence shown by children whose teachers had been told to expect them to show intellectual gains (*dark bars*) and children from whom nothing unusual was expected by their teachers (*light bars*).
(From Rosenthal and Jacobson, 1968)

children do not do well at school if their teachers expect that they will not do well. Rosenthal and Jacobson (1968) gave a test to school children designed to predict 'academic blooming', or so the teachers were led to believe. At the beginning of the following term the teachers were given the names of potential 'bloomers'. These names had in fact been chosen at random, so there was no reason to expect these particular children to put on an intellectual spurt. The results (shown in Figure 2) showed that the 'bloomers' did bloom with the greatest gains being evident in the first grade. It is interesting to note that the children not expected to spurt also showed gains.

As on all those rare occasions when research results strike the imagination, caution must be the rule. Arguments have been put forward that the 'experimenter bias effect' is not as clearly demonstrated as one would like (Barber and Silver, 1968) and it is not found in all situations (Kennedy, 1969). Nonetheless, the weight of evidence favours the idea of an 'experimenter bias' effect.

Rosenthal's suggestion to account for his results is that it is something in the nature of a 'Hawthorne Effect'. This refers to the classic research carried out in the 1920s in a factory in which experiments were conducted to investigate the results of changes in working conditions. The main finding was that, no matter what changes were investigated, whether conditions were made better or worse, output and morale went up. This effect is usually attributed to the interest shown and the attention paid to all of the workers at all times by the experimenters. Equally, coming into school for a University investigation with government money could have the same general effect on the teachers which, in some way, was communicated to the children and encouraged better performance.

Kelly (1955, p. 454) makes the following point about IQ:

The child who is nailed down to the IQ continuum has just that much less chance of changing his teacher's opinion about him. If he is 'low', his unorthodox constructive ventures will never be given a thoughtful hearing; if he is 'high' his stupidities will be indulged as the eccentricities of genius. In formulating the construct of the IQ we may have become enmeshed in the same net that immobilizes many a patient; we may have been caught in the web of our own construct system. Having been so careful to pin all persons down to a continuum with respect to which they can never change, we may now be confronted with a product of our own handiwork – a world full of people whom we cannot conceive of as changing, whom we can do nothing about! Is not IQ a distressingly unfertile construct after all? Should we not, therefore, take better care when we create the design specifications for future diagnostic constructs?

Measuring personal constructs

Measurement has been at the forefront of the psychologist's mind ever since he started to think of himself as a scientist and one of the overriding problems in 'personality' has been to decide what to measure. There has been no such difficulty with construct theory; the unit of measurement is clearly defined – the construct – and Kelly outlined a technique for assessing the mathematical relationship between constructs (repertory grid technique) and a method for obtaining a person's view of himself in qualitative form (self-characterization).

Repertory grid technique

Kelly (1961a) introduced the central idea of the technique in the following way:

Suppose I were to give one of you a card and ask you to write on it the name of your mother. Then I would give you another and ask you to write the name of your father. On a third you might write the name of your wife and on a fourth the name of the girl you almost married – but didn't! We could continue until you had as many as twenty or thirty cards, each showing the name of a person important in your life.

Then suppose I should select three of these cards, perhaps the ones of your father, your mother, and your boss or supervisor. Suppose I should ask you to think of some important way in which any two of them seem to be alike and in contrast to the third. What will you say? Perhaps you will say that your mother and your boss have always seemed to know the answers to the questions you asked but that your father hesitated or told you to seek out your own answers.

Now if this is a distinction you can apply to your father, your mother and your boss, can you extend it also to the other persons you have named? You probably can. The important fact is that as you apply it to person after person you are not only characterizing those persons but you are also providing an operational definition of what you have in mind. Applied to enough persons this operational definition provides a more extensive definition of a particular channel of your thought than do words you may use to symbolize it.

Now suppose I select another three cards, perhaps the ones with the names of your mother, your wife, and the girl you did not marry. What about them? Is there an important way in which two of them – any two – differ from the third? Perhaps you will respond immediately by saying that your wife and your mother are loving but that the girl you did not marry turned out to be harsh.

And how will you extend this personal construct to the other persons who are important in your life? Now let me suppose – for the sake of this discussion – something which I doubt would be true of anyone in this audience. Let me suppose that each person you characterize as 'loving' is a person you have previously characterized as ready to answer your questions, and each person you characterize as 'harsh' is one you previously characterized as sending you off to look for your own answers. Suppose this were true in case after case, on out to infinity. What could we say then? Would we then be ready to say that the two constructs were identical in everything but name?

Not quite! In our illustration the two constructs have been applied only to persons as whole entities. There is still the question of whether the constructs are applied identically to the separate acts of persons. To go even further, this suggests that, in general, the equivalence of constructs is determined by their similar application to all types of events, not merely to human events alone.

Moreover, we need also to make sure that both constructs occupy exactly the same range of convenience. That is to say, can the first construct in my illustration – the response–rejection construct – be applied to all events to which the second construct – the loving–harsh construct – can be applied; and, of course vice versa? If there are some events that can be classified by the person as responsive or rejecting but which he cannot treat in terms of lovingness or harshness, then the ranges of convenience of the two constructs are different and the constructs themselves are therefore not quite the same.

All of this is a mathematical or logical problem and it leads to the formulation of one of the theorems underlying personal construct theory. Since, however, this paper is more concerned with the methodology of personal construct theory than with its mathematics, I shall limit myself to pointing out merely that such propositions exist.

Let us return to our deck of cards. We can represent the data produced so far in a flat matrix with events – in this case the names appearing on the cards – ranged along the top from left to right with the constructs ranged along the side from top to bottom. The entries in the matrix are single digit binary numbers, indicating simply whether the event is regarded one way or the other in terms of the construct. For example, if you regarded your mother as loving, this particular datum would be represented in the matrix by the numeral '1' in the first cell of the second row – below 'mother' and opposite 'loving–harsh'. If you regarded your father as harsh the numeral '0' would be entered in the next cell, etc.

Now we may go on to expand the matrix until it is large enough to give us a stable idea of how the person construes his world. Starting with different triads of cards we can successively produce row after row of matrix entries.

This is not an interminable undertaking. Experience shows that only persons with the most complex or schizoid outlooks require more than twenty or thirty rows to express their repertory of constructs. Repertories used in everyday affairs are generally quite limited and especially, so it appears, among those who prefer to act rather than reflect.

As you can see, the matrix can be factor-analysed to see to what extent the person is employing a variety of constructs, or only a few constructs masquerading under different names. We can examine the columns in the matrix to see which figures in his life are viewed as similar to others, or whether, indeed, there is any great variety perceived among them. For example, does the subject see himself as like his father, or does he see his psycho-therapist as like his father – as psychoanalytic theory suggests he should at certain stages of his treatment?

Incidentally, with regard to this particular psychoanalytic hypothesis, the research does not confirm psychoanalytic thinking. Patients entering into long-term psychotherapy seem rather to view their therapists as more and more like their family physicians.

Again, there are some men who can see complex differences among men, but only one-dimensional differences among women. There are some who have attempted to reduce all their interpersonal relations to the simple structure of one dimension – some military men for example – and there are some who have done this in an effort to control the multi-dimensional confusion of their anxiety.

Research seems to indicate that there are advantages in having a complex repertory of personal constructs, but there are disadvantages too, particularly in decision-making. It appears that schizoid persons have a complex repertory, but that their constructs lack sufficient ranges of convenience to enable the person to relate one of them to another. Thus the system fails to function as a whole and we find erratic sequences in the matrix.

Up to this point we have emphasized the mathematical analysis of the matrix and have ignored the words the person uses to name his constructs. But the words may be examined also. A recent study by Landfield indicates that a verbal analysis distinguishes between university students who are socially well adjusted from those who are not (p values to below ·01), that it sometimes gives a slight prior indication of which maladjusted ones will improve under psychotherapy . . . and that it reflects the degree of improvement of the maladjusted ones under psychotherapy. . . .

But let us turn away from the particular kind of matrix we have described – which, after all, is only one example of the application of the methodology – and look at other kinds of personal construct matrices. Suppose, instead of asking you to write the name of a person on each of the cards I gave you, I would ask you to list an important experience you had had. Suppose, for example, I asked you to think of your wedding and make a note of it on the first card. On the second card you might note the occasion when you had a serious quarrel with your parents, on the third the time when you believed you were near death, on the fourth the ceremony at which you were awarded your university degree, then the meeting when a paper you presented was most severely criticized, and so on. Then suppose you were to construe these events, three at a time as you did the persons in your life, and then extended the constructs to all the other events you had mentioned. This would generate another kind of matrix whose columns and rows, as well as its verbal content, could be analysed.

Or you might list only the catastrophes in your life, and then ask yourself which of the persons you had named could, if they had been available at the time, have been helpful to you in meeting each emergency. Such a matrix provides information about one's allocation of his interpersonal dependencies – whether he has faced difficulties in which he feels no one could be of help, whether he turns to one or two persons only for all kinds of help, or whether he is indiscriminate in his selection of persons upon whom to depend.

Some researchers have used the methodology to come to an understanding of how a young person confronted with making a vocational choice views the different occupations and professions open to him. Others have used it to analyse personal factors in job dissatisfaction. Some have studied changes in the construing process during a year of university training, and others have studied similar changes during psychotherapy (p. 223).

Several other forms of repertory grid have been developed since the one described by Kelly. Specific details of these can be found in Bannister and Mair (1968), but they all have certain general characteristics in common:

1. They are concerned with eliciting the relationships for a person between sets of constructs, either in terms of construing *elements* (as in the Rep Test or the rank order form) or by directly comparing construct with construct (e.g. Hinkle's Impgrid, 1965).

2. The central aim is to reveal the construct patterning for a person and not to relate this patterning to some established normative data. There is no reason why normative data should not be collected for some specific purpose as in the Grid Test of Thought Disorder (Bannister and Frensella, 1966), but the individual construing system is the prime focus and the standard test form an occasionally useful venture.

3. There is no fixed form or content. It is called repertory grid *technique* and not *test* and the selection of the form and content is related to each particular problem. A grid designed to investigate how a nomadic bushman interprets his desert home would be pretty useless to a suburban commuter, even in translation, except perhaps to show that the commuter might have problems if he had to travel in the terrain of the bushman.

4. All forms are designed so that statistical tests of significance can be applied to the set of comparisons each individual has made. A basic assumption underlying the method is that the *psychological* relationships between any two constructs, for a given person, are reflected in the stat-

istical association between them when they are used as judgemental categories.

In its original form the technique was called the Role Construct Repertory Test, and the subject was asked to name twenty or thirty people he knew who fitted different role titles, such as 'teacher you disliked', 'mother', 'person you admire', and these are called *elements*. Constructs were then elicited by selecting three of these elements and asking in what important way two of the people were alike and thereby different from the third. It was from the constructs so elicited that the clinician hoped to gain some insight into the way the person construed his interpersonal environment.

Kelly then modified this to form the Repertory Test, in which the role titles were written along the top of the grid and elicited constructs down the side. It is this form that is described in the quotation from Kelly. In 1959, Bannister showed that misleading correlations could be produced if the ticks and voids in the matrix had a lopsided distribution; if only one person in a matrix was considered an *unprincipled lecher* and one other person was considered a *civil servant*, then there would be a significant correlation between these two constructs because of the unequal distribution of ticks and voids in the matrix. Kelly had been aware of this difficulty and had suggested ways in which lopsided rows could be eliminated. Bannister, however, preferred to modify the technique by forcing the subjects to divide the elements equally between the two poles of the construct. Some people found this method rather artificial and since then it has proved possible to analyse grids in which people have ranked (e.g. *nicest* to *nastiest*) their elements or rated them on seven-point scales.

These forms of grid technique have been used in a variety of ways. Although primarily designed for mapping the unique psychological space of the individual, there are occasions when they are of use in providing group data concerning the construing of specific areas of interest. For instance, if one wanted to investigate the effects of different room arrangements upon people's attitudes towards those rooms, then the grid elements might be pictures of the rooms with different furniture, lighting, shapes, wall surfaces and so forth. Situations rather than people have been used as elements both with adults (Fransella, 1965 and 1971) and with children (Ravenette, 1969). Fransella used speaking situations (e.g. talking on the telephone, to strangers and to those in authority) in studying the construing of 'speaking' of a group of stutterers. Among other things she found that, as might be expected, the likelihood of their stuttering (or more exactly *predicting that they would stutter*) was near certainty if they were feeling anxious or if they had difficulty in seeing or in interpreting the listener's reactions. From this type of grid she showed that a score could be derived that would indicate the 'stuttering-provoking' potential of any given situation for an individual stutterer. This procedure might be of use in de-sensitization treatment which requires that situations be graded from the least to the most troublesome for the person.

Ravenette developed 'situation' grids to avoid the difficulty some children experience in making direct judgements about people. A child chooses a set of pictured situations and then ranks them from say *noisiest* to *quietest*. In a modification of this approach (1970) he has increased the number of elements to sixteen or eighteen and returned to the 'tick versus void' method and added a 'don't know' category. He suggests that the child's use of the 'don't know' category might give some indication of 'a child's willingness to admit to certainty or to defend himself . . .' The results of such grids can be used to increase our understanding of the 'problem child' at school.

Riedel (1970) has attempted to investigate construing by entirely non-verbal means. He has constructed a Personal Construct Inventory which consists of the subject drawing circles within squares of differing dimensions to represent, for instance, the relationship between himself and the world, the self and mother and so forth. The person draws these circles to show relationships under three conditions; self appraisal, other appraisal (i.e. circles drawn the way the person thinks other people such as his mother, would draw them) and ideal appraisal. There is a need for such non-verbal methods for use with people who have never attained language or those who have lost the ability to convey meaning by words – particularly for children, the mentally subnormal and those who have lost speech through damage to the brain. He reports some evidence on the validity and reliability of using spatial rather than verbal tasks to investigate role constructs, but the inventory has yet to be put to experimental use.

A major revision of the theory and technique has been proposed by Hinkle (1965). He saw constructs as being defined by their implications and designed the Implications Grid or Impgrid to quantify these relationships. These grids differ from other forms in that there are no elements to be construed; each construct is paired with every other construct to see which implies the other. There are two sources of information here – one can find out what it means to a person to be a politician and also what things would imply being a politician. That is, a politician may mean being *hard-working, ruthless, two-faced* and *verbally fluent,* though none of these things need *necessarily* imply being a politician.

Hinkle also described a procedure (which he called 'laddering') for finding out the position of any construct or implication in the person's hierarchical construct system. To do this he asked the question 'why'. For each construct elicited, the person is asked which pole of that construct he would prefer to be described by, for example, *verbally fluent* or *a muddled speaker*. If he answers that he would prefer to be *verbally fluent,* he is asked to give his reason for making that choice. If he were to say that people who are *verbally fluent* are *able to get their ideas across* whereas *muddled speakers* only *confuse people,* then *get ideas across – confuse people* is another construct superordinate to the first. He would then be asked why he wanted to *get his ideas across* rather than *to confuse* and he might reply that he would prefer to *get his ideas across* so as *to be admired*. This same process goes on until there is no further answer to the question 'why' – an over-arching principle is reached.

Hinkle tested the superordinancy of these constructs by means of a 'Resistance-to-Change Grid'. In this, the person is presented with pairs of constructs and asked on which he would prefer to remain the same if he were forced to change on one (e.g. would you prefer to change from being *exciting* to *dull* or change from being *verbally fluent* to a *muddled speaker*). He demonstrated that the more resistant to change a construct is, the more likely it is to be superordinate in the hierarchy.

Fransella (1969 and 1971a) has described a modification of an Impgrid in which each pole of a construct can be treated separately so that the implications of each can be established. An example of one such bi-polar Impgrid can be seen in Figure 3. Hinkle had stated that '... the (above) implication hypotheses would lead one to predict that behavioural transformations (slot movement) would occur only on those constructs which have well elaborated networks of implications for both poles of the construct. Indexing the implications of each pole of constructs will facilitate differential predictions with respect to the direction and ease of psychological reconstruction' (Hinkle, 1965, p. 14).

Bannister and Mair conclude their description of Hinkle's work with the following comment:

As a method, Impgrids meet a major requirement of psychological instruments – that they should give the subject maximum freedom to express himself, while still formalizing his contribution to the point at which it can be systematically assessed by the experimenter (Bannister and Mair, 1968, p. 96).

Concepts of reliability and validity

These concepts, concerned with the stability of a measuring instrument and the degree to which it is measuring what one hopes it is measuring, are central to all psychological assessment.

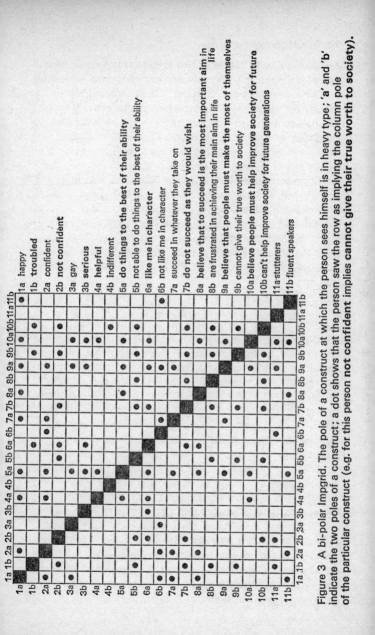

Figure 3 A bi-polar Impgrid. The pole of a construct at which the person sees himself is in heavy type; 'a' and 'b' indicate the two poles of a construct; a dot shows that the person saw the row as implying the column pole of the particular construct (e.g. for this person not confident implies cannot give their true worth to society).

Kelly is reported as referring to reliability as 'a measure of the extent to which a test is insensitive to change'. This is no facetious comment but a logical deduction from his theory which sees man as a form of motion. Mair (1964a and 1964b) has suggested that instead of expecting a measure to yield near identical scores on *all* occasions, one should substitute the notion of *predicting* whether there should or should not be change. Our aim should be to understand the meaning of change, not to regard it as an irritating interference with the 'reliability' of our tests by an irresponsible subject – to be looked on as 'error variance'.

There can, of course, be no such thing as *the* reliability of repertory grid technique, since there is no one form of the grid. At the end of a long and detailed discussion of reliability in relation to grid method, Bannister and Mair conclude:

One practical rule must be that if the reliability of a particular grid in a particular context needs to be known, for either theoretical or practical reasons, then it will have to be specifically assessed as part of the experimental venture. It is to be hoped that the day of the comprehensive cookbook of tables of grid reliabilities will never come. Such a volume might help perpetuate the tendency to regard high reliability as an experimental necessity, rather than encourage the view that 'reliability' is, in itself, a target for experimental investigation (Bannister and Mair, 1968, p. 175).

Reliability coefficients can, indeed, be useful sources of information. They can, and have been, used as scores. Bannister (1962) showed that not only did schizophrenics who were thought-disordered relate constructs as if each were a virtually separate dimension, but they were inconsistent in their use of these dimensions on a second occasion. Some so-called 'normal' subjects also seem to use constructs as near discrete entities, but they use them with relative consistency. Thus, degree of consistency shown on immediate retest was used as one of the scores in a test designed to identify the type of thought disorder found in some schizophrenics (Bannister and Fransella, 1966 and 1967).

Kelly is reported as having defined validity as 'the capacity of a test to tell us what we already know'. A recent rider to this was provided by Dolliver (1969). He reviewed the literature on the widely used Strong Vocational Interest Blank (SVIB), which is designed to help fit round-peg humans into round-peg jobs, and he found evidence suggesting that asking the person concerned what he wanted to do on leaving college was a *better* predictor of what the person finally did than was the SVIB. Asking a person what he wants to do in the way of work in the future may be more informative than getting him to fill in an oblique questionnaire.

Vernon says he takes an unorthodox stand in thinking that 'a test measures only itself, but that it is valid in so far as it can be shown to correlate with other observable behaviour. That is, its validity lies in the inference we are entitled to make from it' (Vernon, 1964, p. 213).

An increasing number of studies show that a variety of valid inferences can be drawn from grid data. For instance, the degree of empathy between client and clinician was related to improvement in psychotherapy when empathy was defined as the similarity between the patient's self-description and the therapist's description of the patient (Cartwright and Lerner, 1963). Similarly, improvement was found to be related to the degree to which the therapist understands the patient's construct system (Landfield and Nawas, 1964). Mair (1966) demonstrated that it was possible to predict simple grid relationships for pairs of constructs on a 'dictionary' basis. Knowles and Purves (1965) found that attitude to the experimenter and need for approval, as measured by grids, was related to the ease with which subjects responded to verbal conditioning.

In 1967 Fransella and Bannister reported that it was possible to predict the voting behaviour of people from a knowledge of the relationship between evaluative constructs and party labels. For instance, the way the subjects rank-ordered the elements (people they individually knew) in terms of *like I'd like to be in character* was compared with the way the elements were ranked on the constructs *likely to vote Conservative, likely to vote Labour* and *likely to vote Liberal*. The more closely a person (in grid terms) identified his ideal view of himself with a generalized view of members of a particular political party, the more likely he was to vote for that party. It was also possible to identify something similar to a 'brand image' flavour in the results. Both Labour and Conservative voters agreed that Conservatives were *proud of being British,* but Labour supporters associated this *positively* and significantly with being *prejudiced* and Conservatives *negatively* with being *prejudiced.* Although one may get predicted relationships between pairs of constructs, the relationship between these and the total construct system may vary considerably between individuals. Brand X may be a much *nicer smelling* male deodorant than brand Y, but male deodorants may be construed by some as *effeminate* and therefore *undesirable.*

Single case studies have suggested that construct relationships are meaningfully linked to what is known about single individuals and that certain predictable patternings occur (e.g. Salmon, 1963; Fransella and Adams, 1965; Bannister and Mair, 1968). These latter authors point out that future work on single cases could be along the following lines.

Probably the most useful, if not the most frequent, ventures will be those in which the grid is used with a single patient where the approach has formal coherence, so that predictions are made before test, the lines of treatment appropriate to negation or support of the hypotheses are specified before test, and the criteria of successful outcome of these predictions are defined in advance (Bannister and Mair, 1968, p. 200).

Self-characterization

Kelly many times insisted that he would prefer to be remembered, if at all, not for the invention of personal construct theory but for 'Kelly's first principle'. Kelly's first principle was the simple statement 'if you don't know what is wrong with the patient, ask him, he *may* tell you'. It seems likely that out of this joke Kelly invented (and he was prone to invent things very fruitfully out of jokes) the technique of person assessment which he called *self-characterization*. It is interesting that psychologists seem always to have been suspicious of the value of direct personal statements. They make their tests oblique so that what is being measured is obscured from the subject. They embed lie scales in their questionnaires on the assumption that man is a deceiving creature. Yet many of us might feel that we have something meaningful (perhaps even scientifically meaningful) to say concerning ourselves and what we have been about. Self-characterization is a format which invites the person to say something about himself.

The person is invited to portray himself in the following way.

I want you to write a character sketch of Harry Brown, just as if he were the principal character in a play. Write it as it might be written by a friend who knew him very *intimately* and very *sympathetically*, perhaps better than anyone ever really could know him. Be sure to write it in the third person. For example, start out by saying 'Harry Brown is . . ." '.

This wording was designed to reduce any threat to a minimum and encourage an overall assessment of the person by himself in as objective a way as possible. The aim is to find out how the person structures his immediate world, how he sees *himself* in relation to these structures and the strategies he has developed to handle his world.

The following is a self-characterization written by a patient in a psychiatric hospital.

Do you know Mr Smith John? I do not. Only the other day he was walking down Marvels Lane to work. He can certainly walk, I have known Mr Smith to walk for miles John, sometimes to save a sixpenny bus fare. When you meet him in the street, he does not say much to you if hardly anything, he always seems to be in a hurry to go wherever he is going.

Have you seen his paintings of landscapes and trees? When he first began to paint he used to walk through the woods making sketches of trees, you know he loves trees, sometimes more than people, we should stop to think sometimes about people but he seems to show more affection and love for things and places, anything that cannot hurt him back or take anything away from him. He spent hours in that cold bedroom of his painting and waiting for the paint to dry. But he told me that there were other attractions in the woods, besides drawing trees and try as he might not to, it was looking at courting couples lying on the grass. He told me he used to go home and masturbate himself at what he had seen, then he would feel this deep guilt which would destroy any creative art he had in him. He would come to hate the courting couples because it would destroy his concentration in the woods and the creative spirit he wanted to draw trees and landscapes, and you know John some of his pictures were sometimes lovely, he has sold some, but he mostly gave them away to the school where his children go because they wanted to show their teachers and say 'my Dad done that'.

There is also his music John have you heard him play the accordion, the will power that man must have to start playing the accordion at forty-three, but as was said before the love he gives to things is unbelievable. His wife told me that he is always sweeping up and tidying the house and that he hates to see the children make a mess in the home, sometimes he gets very annoyed if they disturb him when he is practising. But even with his music, he gets that tremendous sexual urge to go out again and do all those things he hates doing, then he is lost for music, painting and anything creative that is deep inside him. But you know John a man like him must always be doing something then he is happy. But you also know John when he is happy and contented and creating he is a most agreeable person to get on with, but if you hurt him, he is not and seems to lose control of his speech and say horrible and nasty things, which he does not mean. Well John I must go, if you see Mr Smith give him my regards.

Suppose now instead of rushing off to count the verb to adjective ratio or even the number of threat to non-threat words we look in fairly direct terms at what the person has said. Perhaps we ought to pay particular attention to the opening statement of any self-characterization, because it seems likely that a person might try to pin-point some central issue, set the tone and announce his general purpose right at the beginning. 'Mr Smith began by asking a question of the psychologist: 'Do you know Mr Smith?' He immediately answered it for himself: 'I do not'. We could take this as an announcement of what, in jargon terms, might be called 'an identity problem' and then consider if this is a reasonable statement of his central theme. Truly, the rest of the self-characterization describes a man isolated from other people to the point where they are a menace because they interfere with his understanding of things and love of things. If the construct theory assertion that we come to understand ourselves via our understanding of other people (sociality corollary) is valid, then it seems quite likely that this man would be a mystery to himself. Apparently he has tried to understand himself by staring at his own navel rather than accepting that we see ourselves reflected in the eyes of other people.

We might look at the sequence of statements to observe the contrasts that are being drawn. This is a man in a great hurry, so that he says nothing to you but speeds on by and yet, in relation to 'things', he will spend hours in that cold bedroom of his, waiting for the paint to dry.

We might note the sequence of cause and effect as it is understood by the writer. An innocent stroll in the woods to enjoy the painter's view of things causes you to see men and women loving each other which causes you to masturbate which causes you to feel guilt which destroys your creative capacity as a painter.

We might note any tentative modifications to the general rules laid down. We play the accordion not for anyone else, only for ourselves, because it shows our determination and competence. Yet however casually we sell or give away our pictures, we do note the reaction of others to them.

Kelly (1955, p. 315) deals at some length with methods of analysing self-characterizations but suggests no methods for quantifying their content. A step in the direction of organizing this mass of information in content terms is Landfield's manual for categorizing constructs (1965 and 1967). But perhaps the most significant feature of the invention of the self-characterization is the recognition that a man's view of himself may be materially more worth our consideration as psychologists than his interpretation of our clever ink blots or his answers to the semi-relevant questions which we have concocted for our questionnaires.

The measure of man

Kelly summarized the construct theory view of man thus:

What I think this view of man as the paradigm of the scientist – and vice versa – does mean is that the ultimate explanation of human behavior lies in scanning man's undertakings, the questions he asks, the lines of inquiry he initiates and the strategies he employs, rather than in analysing the logical pattern of the events with which he collides. Until one has grasped the nature of man's undertakings, he can scarcely hope to make sense out of the muscular movements he observes or the words he hears spoken. In dealing with human behavior we inevitably find ourselves confronted with the human ingenuity it expresses. And that is the point of confrontation at which most psychology breaks down (Kelly, 1969, p. 16).

Perhaps then our signal failure to measure the person derives from our habit of asking him to answer our questions rather than noting the nature of the questions which *he* is asking.

A change to a psychology of inquiring man might additionally guard us from the danger of trying to turn our *descriptions of* man into *prescriptions for* man. Leman (1970a) stresses this sinister potential of scientism in the following terms.

What I want to suggest here, is that many scientific theories (and not least some of those contrapted by psychologists) are not up to much as explanations of past events but are highly significant as programmes for future events of a kind to suit the originating scientist.

(Something of the same sort goes on in advertisements: if you say, or show, that all considerable people are seen alive with your product, you are not reporting this as a fact recorded by the angel, you are trying to make it happen. You may remember the whisky poster which said nothing but 'Haig in Every Home'.)
... What I have been saying, is that I don't believe learning theory is correct as an explanation of things that have happened,

of what you and I did yesterday, or last time a psychologist happened to be looking; that I think learning theory assumes, not man as he is and has hitherto been, but the ideal type of mechanarchic man; it doesn't really say what you are like, it says what They (namely, *hypocrite lecteur*, Us with Our hat on) would like you to be like; and that's fair warning that they will make you like that if they can.

Everybody capable of entertaining the thought now knows that psychology is a branch of politics, mainly concerned with disposal of bodies and the dispensing of existence: who is right, who wrong; who is to get the schooling and subsequent gravy; who not?

All through man's history he has been subject to attempts (ranging from massive experiments by Genghis Khan and Nero on to the work of Torquemada and Himmler) to make him jump to a punishment and reward schedule. Psychologists cannot really be non-aligned on such issues.

4 The Development of the Person

Larry and I had a conversation about hunting during which I mentioned that pygmies used darts dipped in poison for hunting and for defence. This intrigued Larry. Half an hour later he approached me with a stick and jabbed it into my leg.

'There, Don, she's dead.'

I slumped over, playing my part in the game. Larry became very excited and shouted:

'Let's bury her, Don!' As he tried to pick me up I collapsed on the floor and Larry started shovelling imaginary sand on top of me. Sally came into the room and, finding me 'dead', threw her arms around my neck and started to cry. I reassured her, and then noticed Larry curled up on the floor behind me.

'I wonder what you are doing?'

'I'm just lying here feeling sorry for you, Mrs Upton.'

GEORGE A. KELLY
Behaviour is an Experiment

People interpret and re-interpret themselves and their situation. The whole of construct theory is based upon this fundamental idea that a person's psychological processes are channelled by the ways in which he successively construes events. Viewing man in relation to a time line, changing from moment to moment, probably never absolutely the same from one second to the next, is an unusual vision in psychology. It accepts that since every man is 'developing' or changing from the moment he is born, he can indeed be seen as a form of motion. If we follow this line of thought, then it becomes less meaningful to divide people up into arbitrary 'stages of development' such as childhood, adolescence, adulthood and old age; or, within the childhood bracket, oral, anal, genital and so forth.

Salmon (1970) pointed out that psychological theorizing about stages – and other aspects of the child – has had a profound influence on the ways in which parents have brought up their children; behaviourism led to rigorous time tabling of living, everything metered according to a schedule; Freudianism led to an anxious concern about the probably harmful effects if the parent did not adopt the 'proper' emotional stance towards the child. Today parents have perhaps less guidance from the 'experts' on how to bring up their children, now it is the turn of teachers to be influenced by psychological theory. Piaget's theory of cognitive development in the child is having profound effects on teaching methods. Kelly and Piaget have much in common, including the conviction that human beings should be regarded as, say, 'thinkers' rather than 'organisms' or 'computers' or entirely bound by their 'unconscious dynamics'. Both argued that if we listen credulously to what people, child or adult, say, then we may start to understand why they approach life in the way they do.

It was a great misfortune that Kelly died before he made more explicit his views on the early development of construct systems. As it stands, the theory can potentially deal with the psychology of the child. There is however a great deal to be explored about the ways in which the constructs a child uses change as he grows older – in organization, in permeability, in form *and* in content.

One can apply construct theory to the child *in utero* quite easily, providing one remembers that constructs need not be verbal, but can be pre-verbal discriminations. A construct is essentially a discrimination between things that are similar and thereby different from other things and it is a foetal discrimination between an oxygenated and an oxygen-starved environment that precipitates him into being a 'child'.

It is not argued that a child recognizes (in the sense of being able to articulate) differences and similarities, but that his discrimination is not fundamentally different from that evinced by an adult when we ask him to tell us which two of the sounds of a fog horn, a siren and a penny whistle are alike and thereby different from the third.

Piaget

Many of Piaget's experiments showing the development of the concepts of time, number or movement, can be seen as examples of how the child may develop the ability to construe certain events in the way others in his culture construe them, e.g. acquire a superordinate construction about the conservation of mass. Piaget's constructs about the stages through which a child psychologically evolves are derived from conventional discourse about reasoning and logic – concrete, formal, egocentric, reciprocal and so forth. They could be transformed into construct theory terms (reciprocality equals the development of role construing, concretism equals the use of subordinate constructs with only simple and inflexible links to superordinates, e.g. *ice cream* versus *no ice cream* implies *good* versus *bad*). But there are substantial differences in the two approaches. A construct theorist would see the stages as related to experience (serial reconstruction) not age, he would seek to construe and measure changes in structural rather than culture-content terms.

Additionally, in spite of many theoretical similarities between the Piagetian and Kellian view, Salmon points to their divergence in underlying philosophical assumptions:

Piaget's theoretical account rests on an absolute view of truth. Assimilation, one half of the adaptation process, is defined as shaping outer reality to the inner conceptual world, while accommodation, the other half, represents a modification of the inner world to fit the demands of outer reality. Underlying such an account is the assumption that a person can directly experience pure reality and can distinguish between this and his inner conceptual world. This view runs counter to the philosophical basis of construct theory, whereby reality can never be known in any final, absolute way, but only through our constructions which, as a result of the varying validational outcomes of the behavioural experiments we make, are subject to continual revision (Salmon, 1970, p. 214).

A construct theory approach to development

Salmon further points out that Piaget's theoretical model is primarily concerned with the development of thinking about the physical world and has little to say about the development of the person *qua* person. She suggests that the development of personality in the child can be seen in terms of the Kellian view of role. The child's construing of his mother's construct system is the jumping off ground for the development of the child's construing system. He starts out with this and uses it in his dealings with others. Soon he meets others like himself and finds that all the anticipations he makes do not always work out, so he develops new role constructs in relation to others of his age. So he goes on, gradually elaborating his role construing. Perhaps the traditional Oedipus complex could be seen in the light of the child reaching an age when father expects child to construe some of *his* constructs. The child may find that some of these conflict with those developed in relation to his mother and so he shows hostility by 'acting the baby', or aggression – he actively elaborates his system to incorporate some of his father's constructs. Development can be seen as occurring largely when anticipations fail. The over-protected child may never be put into a position where using the constructions his mother puts on events leads to invalidation. He fails to 'develop' as an individual.

Fransella (1971a) has suggested that construct theory be applied to explain the development of some forms of behaviour that are considered abnormal, such as stuttering. If a child's early constructs are developed as he construes the construction processes of his mother, as suggested by Salmon, then we come near to the explanation of stuttering propounded by Johnson (1942). His theory was that most children have some form of speech disfluency as they learn to talk but that a child will only become a stutterer if his parents are particularly concerned by speech defects and come to construe him a stutterer. In construct theory terms, we have the child looking at and organizing his world largely through the eyes of his mother. His mother is, for some reason, concerned about speech and the disfluencies exhibited by the child. The child comes then to construe his own speech in terms of concern. His discriminations concerning speech will be largely pre-verbal and of a tentative nature. He will try out different ways of speaking – such as slowly, trying to get it all out in a rush, taking a deep breath and so forth. He will observe the effects of these experiments on his mother and modify his speech according to the reaction he perceives. What seems to be happening is that this child is developing a network of constructs and implications to do with *his speech,* and this happens to be, at that age, disfluent speech. It follows that the stuttering child should have far more constructs to do with the speaking situation than the child who is not called a stutterer. It is argued that the thing that keeps him stuttering is his inability to construe his *fluencies* and so construe himself as a normal speaker.

The developing construct system

Salmon (1970) considers that one of the major aspects of a developing construct system is the increasing degree of organization of the system, in terms of superordinacy. Educational growth is not the accumulation of more and more pieces of information, but the development of an increasingly complex structure for organizing and inter-relating ideas. If this notion were followed, then some of the traditional boundaries between 'subjects' at school would cease to exist (consider an Eng. Lit., History, Current Affairs, Geography merger). The present system favours the development of the dread disease which Kelly referred to as 'hardening of the categories' rather than the elaborating of a network of meanings.

In terms of organization of construing it seems likely that some areas involving the construing of people will be more difficult at earlier age levels than those concerned with the construing of objects. There is regrettably little evidence as to the specific processes that take place during the hierarchical development of construct systems. What little information there is suggests that children move from using physicalistic constructs to using psychological ones (Little, 1968) and that psychological constructs increase in complexity with age (Brierley, 1967).

Brierley elicited constructs from ninety boys and girls from working and middle-class homes and at ages seven, ten and thirteen. She categorized the constructs in the following ways.

1. Kinship, e.g. *these are not in our family.*
2. Social role, e.g. *these are children.*
3. Appearance, e.g. *these are on the skinny side.*
4. Behaviour, e.g. *these play musical instruments.*
5. Personality, e.g. *these are nosey.*
6. Literal, e.g. *these have the same Christian name.*

Table 1 shows how the percentage of these categories varied across ages.

Table 1

Percentage of Six types of Construct Elicited from Children in Three Age Groups

Type of construct	Percentage at age		
	7	10	13
Kinship	2·9	2·7	1·3
Social role	29·5	26·9	8·8
Appearance	32·3	30·6	8·9
Behaviour	24·3	31·0	41·3
Personality	9·8	18·4	39·7
Literal	0·2	0·0	0·0

Source: Brierley (1967)

Both behavioural and personality constructs increased in number with age and all others decreased except for kinship constructs which showed no variation. Personality constructs showed the greatest increase. Overall, at seven years children were using kinship and social role constructs, at ten years appearance and behaviour constructs and at thirteen years, personality constructs, but a breakdown into sex groups showed that girls used appreciably more personality constructs than boys. At the age of thirteen, girls were using personality constructs in preference to all other kinds, while boys were using behaviour constructs. Dividing the children up on the basis of social class showed that working-class boys were using more personality constructs than middle-class boys at ages ten and thirteen, and working-class girls more than middle-class girls at age ten.

Kelly stressed the notion of construct *subsystems*. One subsystem may be highly developed and organized, enabling accurate predictions to be made in that area of construing, and another subsystem may be poorly elaborated. For instance, it is possible for an individual to have a highly developed system to do with physics that enables him to incorporate any new 'physics' event within his existing framework. Yet, when dealing with people, his role construing can be so impoverished that he stands out like a sore thumb in a social gathering, unable to establish a social relationship with anybody. The whole tradition of work on intelligence can be seen as an excessive concern with the development of particular subsystems.

Creativity

Hudson (1970) has shown that boys, quite early on, develop a stereotype of a 'Science' and an 'Arts' boy, and that those who commit themselves to Science do so much earlier than those who commit themselves to Arts. This dichotomy is linked also with *ways* of thinking – convergent or divergent. The converger is good at conventional intelligence tests; specializes in physical sciences; holds conventional attitudes; has mechanical or technical hobbies; and is emotionally inhibited. In contrast, the diverger is best at tests that do not have single answers; specializes in arts subjects or biology;

holds unconventional attitudes; his interests mainly centre upon people; he is emotionally uninhibited (Hudson, 1968).

Hudson carried out an experiment in which he *instructed* boys in such a way that they were encouraged to think divergently. The result was a great increase in the number of suggested uses for three objects in a modified version of the Uses of Objects test.

The converger, in other words, is not so much the boy who cannot think divergently, as the one who thinks fluently only when told unambiguously to do so.... This is not to say that the divergent capacities of all boys are identical. High scorers on the first condition tend to be high scorers on the second. Rather, it seems that the fluency of most boys can be made to vary over quite a wide range; and many have reserves of mental fluency that under normal circumstances they keep to themselves (Hudson, 1970, p. 85).

Not only instructions can influence results. A further experiment showed how the 'Artist' boy can act the 'Scientist' boy and *vice versa*. Boys were given similar versions of a creativity test to do in three roles – once as themselves, once as a character sketched as a bohemian artist, and once as if they were a character fitting the stereotype of a scientist. The boys, when playing the role of a scientist, gave typical 'scientist' responses, emphasizing practicality and ingenuity; when playing the role of the 'artist' they produced much more flamboyant responses. The boys produced more responses both in quantity and diversity when they were playing the role of someone *other* than themselves.

What are the implications of such experiments? Rosenthal and Jacobson (1968) showed how the 'intelligence' of children can be raised by the expectations of their teachers. Hudson demonstrated how instructions and the context within which a test is administered can affect results – convergers can think divergently when they are encouraged to take a 'divergent' role. But the extent to which this becomes less possible with increasing age is not known. It may be that when the 'converger' role becomes a way of life in which the individual has invested a great deal, his ability to play the role of a divergent thinker lessens.

It is interesting to speculate about what the possible long-term effects of current changes in teaching method might be. Children from nursery school onwards are being taught to think divergently, to think up more and more alternative ways of construing things or events. Perhaps this in turn is related to the decreasing number of children who are interested in science subjects in secondary schools. If a nation of divergent thinkers emerges, there might be no more 'scientists' in the very limited sense of the term. Of course 'divergence' and 'convergence' are not traits, but merely, perhaps, a person's first publicly approved method of approach to a problem. A more divergent culture might more clearly recognize that the best science has always been an adventurous act of imagination and the successful scientist has surely to indulge in both types of thinking alternatively. He thinks divergently to create his hypotheses and convergently to formulate these hypotheses so that they can be tested.

Construct theory includes the idea of a Creativity Cycle: this 'is one which starts with loosened construction and terminates with tightened and validated construction'. A scientist or a person who always indulges in tight construing may have a massive concrete output to his credit, but will never be able to produce new ideas since creative thinking can only result from loosening the connections between constructs and realigning them in an unusual way. On the other hand, a person who thinks loosely all the time cannot be creative either, since he is unable to tighten up his ideas to the point where he can see what he has got and evaluate it. In the end, there has to be a hypothesis to test – either by formal experiment or by living it. Hudson's convergently-thinking scientist, then, is someone who specializes in the use of tight construing; he minimizes the importance of letting his intellectual hair down. But this does not mean he cannot 'loosen', it may only mean that people he considers important consistently validate his constructions when he adopts a

'tight' posture. That it is something of a role is further suggested by the finding of Hudson, that boys do not see themselves as belonging exclusively to either 'scientist' or 'arts' role
types; they see themselves as having the good qualities of
both. This opting the self out of a stereotype can be observed
in a number of social and psychotherapeutic contexts.

The extent to which a child emphasizes the value of particular stages in the Creativity Cycle will depend on his experiences at home and at school and the value placed on
each stage by his parents and teachers. Hudson reports
results suggesting that divergent teachers do best with divergent boys and convergent teachers with convergent boys –
but this can be taken as evidence of the self-fulfilling
prophecy in trait psychology – trait 'laws' tend to become
prescriptions.

Personal problems

One of the many problems encountered by teachers is that
of the child who is not learning to read as he should. Many
teachers seek the explanation for such failure in the defects
of the child and not in his interaction with home and school
(Ravenette, 1968). The most popular explanation given by
teachers was that of lack of intelligence, which tends to
imply that there is little that can be done. Ravenette reports
how Kelly was once asked how his theory related to the
problem of a child failing to learn to read and how he replied: 'Find out if the child likes the teacher'. Such an
answer suggests changing the emphasis from 'why is the
child not *able* to read?' to 'why does the child not *want* to
read?' An investigation of how the child views his school and
his home environment and his idea of what 'reading' is about
may provide explanations of the child's reluctance to do
what others do. For example, a child may have experienced
persistent failure – perhaps at nursery school, perhaps in
relation to an elder, clever brother, or his parents' expectations – and come to see himself as a failure. Having construed himself as a failure (either generally or more
specifically in relation to reading) then there must be some

problematical implications for him of being a success. Ravenette points out that these implications of success are likely to be very important and need to be identified if progress is to be made. They may relate to another personal dimension potentially troublesome for the child – that of growing up – and learning to read is part of growing up. Perhaps his perception of adult life has not been a happy one and he has witnessed cruelty and unhappiness which makes adulthood look an extremely undesirable state.

Ravenette suggests other personal dimensions along which a child's reading 'problem' can be looked at and adds corollaries to Kelly's statement as follows:

Find out if the teacher, or parent, likes the child, and at the same time is not forcing the child into a role which is inappropriate, and is not depriving the child of the means of developing his own identity in a constructive way, nor using the child to meet his own needs (Ravenette, 1968, p. 77).

The educational system

Construct theory has implications for the educational process itself. Children being taught arithmetic are shown methods for dealing with numbers in certain ways so as to get certain types of answers. They then move on to another subject, say algebra, to learn other ways of dealing with numbers. But what of the child who has found that arithmetical procedures are quite adequate for solving all the problems with which he has been presented? If at the end of his arithmetic course he had been presented with problems with which his arithmetic construing system could not deal, the experience of invalidation might have encouraged him to view algebra as a salvation rather than a pointless exercise. The experience of being 'wrong' is educationally as important as the experience of being 'right'.

It may be that the whole developmental cycle is best maintained as a continuous movement, by alternating the experiences of validation and invalidation. Bannister (1965) found that people tend to tighten the relationship between constructs when they experience validation and loosen when invalidated. Elaboration occurs when constructs are sufficiently loosely related to deal with new experiences. In the context of group psychotherapy (a truly educational context) it was found that construing systems loosened before people radically changed their views of one another (Fransella & Joyston-Bechal, 1971). Kelly has argued that the elaboration of the way a person understands and interprets the world is achieved by alternating between tight and loose construing. When we construe tightly, our constructs are few in number, closely related and well-articulated and our expectations are specific and concrete. When we construe loosely, our constructs are many, vaguely related and only partly verbalized and our expectations are broad and approximate. Thus we range between 'facts' and 'dreams'. A few brass tacks rescue us from schizophrenia – a fantasy or two safeguards us from obsessionality. Neither tight nor loose construing is good in itself – development is a word for movement between the two.

That loose-to-tight-to-loose construing is a normal, if submerged, aspect of education is indicated by the work of Runkel and Damrin (1961). They showed that teacher-training students who were at the beginning of training (measured in terms of their mastery of their subject) were using a multiplicity of loosely related dimensions in terms of which to view children. At a mid-point in training, students had narrowed down to a simple tight view using only a few dimensions. Towards the end of training the students again loosened their subsystem. Success as a teacher seemed to relate to the distance moved from loose-to-tight-to-loose rather than to being solely one or the other.

Development as a perpetual experiment

In construct theory terms, reading is a new adventure for the child, but he will only embark on this adventure if he thinks the quest worth undertaking. In 'Behaviour is an experiment', Kelly describes a school run along lines suggested by personal construct theory.

The primary object of the school is not to control behaviour, or even to 'give' the child experience – two goals frequently cited by educators. In a society convinced that freedom is more than a happy personal convenience, that it also enables men to make the most of their capacity to help each other, a school cannot allow itself to become an instrument for keeping the under-privileged in line by squelching their impulses. Moreover, the school cannot permit itself to take the position that experience, instead of being a prerogative of all human life, is to be doled out in calculated amounts by the educational establishment. Yet none of this is to say that limits on behaviour are to be abandoned or that experience cannot proceed in an orderly fashion....

The limits on behaviour are seen as largely self-imposed by the child; but regardless of who imposes them, they serve as guard-rails permitting freer experimentation within presumed limits of safety. Occasionally one finds the limits have been set altogether too far out and a child shrinks back from exploration. Some-times they are set too close in and he explores coherently only within infantile orbits. When he must function outside the limits, his behaviourally posed questions are observed to be frantic and his experiments inconclusive (Kelly, 1970b, pp. 261–2).

In order to take part in the child's experimentation, the teacher must get some idea of what is being seen through the child's eyes; she must 'enact a role'. Mrs Upton, the head of the school, sees fantasy play as one of the ways in which children role-play parts that are beyond their self-imposed limits, so that they can see what there is beyond those limits. She actively participates in these games her children play and suggests experimental roles they might adopt that will lead to the elaboration of their construct systems.

This notion of experimenting man seems eminently appli-cable to the so-called 'adolescent problem' – a problem for adults, not for adolescents. They can be seen as experi-menting, as actively elaborating their construct systems (showing aggression in the Kellian sense). The question for the adults becomes one of 'why do they need to experiment so actively?' If there were a different emphasis in our schools, each child might be enabled to ask his own personal questions, rather than simply be part of a standard class apparently asking the same questions.

As an example of the more extreme attitudes pervading our educational system consider these words from an open letter to MPs:

The new fashionable anarchy flies in the face of human nature, for it holds that children and students will work from natural inclination rather than the desire for reward. . . .

Exams make people work hard. Much opposition to them is based on the belief that people work better without reward and incentive, a naïveté which is against all knowledge of human nature. All life depends upon passing exams. If you fail at football, they drop you to the reserves. If you fail in business you go bankrupt. If you fail in politics, you are forced to resign (or, in some countries, get shot). To create an education system without examinations is to fail to prepare children and students for the realities of adult life (Cox and Dyson, 1969).

Is it not against constructs like these that the youth of today is rebelling? They are challenging, among other things, the premise that 'all life depends upon passing exams' and the pre-emptive view of 'human nature' expressed. They do not see why life needs to be competitive – they are experimenting with opting out and the answers they get from society will help determine what future questions they ask.

'Problem' children

Some youths behave in such a way that society dictates that they need 'correction'. One or two studies have tried to find out who delinquents identify with. At the time of being sent to a training school the delinquents seemed to lack identification with authority figures but to identify strongly with their delinquent pals. During the training period, they became more identified with authority figures and less with other delinquents.

In a study designed to show differences between groups of delinquent boys rather than how they differ from non-delinquents (Holland, 1971), boys were required to fill out a questionnaire, once as themselves and again as other people might fill it out. The questionnaire was designed to measure 'powerlessness'. Recent opinion (e.g. Gold, 1969) considers that youths take part in delinquent acts as a reaction to feelings of powerlessness. Holland found that the boys as a whole *did* see themselves as significantly less powerful than people having high status, such as doctor, policeman, school teacher and prime minister. Less obvious was her finding that boys who abscond see these figures as relatively *less* powerful than did non-absconders. This is an example of how behaviour is a form of question. The act of absconding can be seen as the question: 'What exactly is the extent of *their* power?' or 'Are they as lacking in power as I think they are?' Holland found a kind of realistic hopelessness in both groups of delinquents. They recognized the height of the power pyramid above them in that they saw policemen as being relatively powerless. They additionally saw policemen as believing that people 'can't change very much'. If we come to believe that we cannot change no matter what we do, then presumably our behaviour must become repetitious indeed.

Development – opera not overture

Construct theory offers many new ways of thinking about development, that is, development in the traditional psychological sense of 'birth to adolescence'. Of course construct theory is a theory of perpetual development even though we sometimes ask questions of our environment that help us only to paint ourselves into a corner. It makes us think of the child as a person rather than as 'savage' or 'computer' or 'mini-adult'. It has implications for the education process itself and it particularly emphasizes the importance of the child's interpretation of his environment. It makes us concern ourselves with the development of psychological processes rather than with arbitrary stages or traits. Lastly it has implications for the child who has problems, be they 'educational' or 'behavioural' or 'personal' – remembering that these are our categories not the child's.

5 Person to Person

... the Variations have amused me because I've labelled 'em with the nicknames of my particular friends – *you* are Nimrod. That is to say I've written the variations each one to represent the mood of the 'party' – I've liked to imagine the 'party' writing the variation him (or her) self and have written what I think they would have written – if they were asses enough to compose – it's a quaint idea and the result is amusing to those behind the scenes and won't affect the hearer who 'nose nuffin'.
EDWARD ELGAR, letter to a friend

Of all the many curious divisons in psychology, perhaps the strangest is that termed 'social psychology'. Strange because, unless one is a hermit, the vast majority of what people do takes place within a social context; even construing a man as a hermit has a social referent – being *not* social.

The psychological experiment

Contrary to popular belief, the official psychological experiment also takes place within a social setting, even down to the rat that performs differently if it has experienced 'gentling' (an academic way of saying that it has been handled and stroked, e.g. Levine, 1956). The 'experimenter-subject' can be be looked on as yet another example of a role relationship.

Rosenthal (1967) talks of various effects that can occur between an experimenter and his subject. Studies of *biosocial* effects include the finding that female subjects are smiled at 70 per cent of the time while males receive smiles on only 15 per cent of occasions; experimenters take more time to collect data from females than from males; young subjects are less likely to say 'unacceptable' things to older experimenters; Negroes control their hostility more with white than with Negro experimenters. *Situational* effects include the findings that experienced experimenters obtain different responses from those with less experience; those who know the subjects get different results from those who test strangers. One of Rosenthal's best known ideas is that of the 'experimenter bias' effect. This refers to the basic fact that in most research the experimenter has some expectations as to the outcome of the study. An example of this was given in the previous chapter. When teachers expected children to put on an intellectual spurt, they did so more markedly than did the children of whom nothing outstanding was expected. Many other experiments have now beeen conducted to show this effect. In one of Rosenthal's laboratory experiments all experimenters were given the same instructions on how to carry out a study in which subjects judged the expressions on faces in ten photographs. Half the experimenters were told that previous research had shown the 'well established fact' that people rated the photographs as those of 'successful' people, while the other group were told that the judges tended to rate them as 'unsuccessful'. Experimenters who were led to expect that their subjects would judge the photographs to be those of 'successful' people did, in fact, obtain higher ratings of success from these subjects than did the 'unsuccessful' experimenters.

Milgram (1965) showed clearly that quite ordinary people are willing to inflict severe pain in the form of electric shocks in a laboratory experiment when they are officially told that they are the 'experimenter'. He demonstrated that the farther away 'authority' was, the less obedient to instructions was the 'experimenter'. Some reduced the level of shocks given when the psychologist was out of the room and lied about this when the psychologist returned. Additionally, the nearer 'psychologically' the subject was to his victim, the less willing he was to participate. If he had to come close or touch the 'victim' the more likely he was to be disobedient, but if the 'victim' were in another room, it was apparently easier to inflict pain. The fact that this was play-acting on the 'victim's' part (he was pretending to be writhing in agony at the shock, but no shock was actually received) does not alter the fact that these people thought they were inflicting pain and were prepared to do so *within a social experimental setting* and that variations in the social setting varied their willingness to participate.

Rosenthal's category of psychosocial effects includes studies showing that 'researchers higher in status – a professor as compared to a graduate student, or a captain as compared to a corporal – tend to obtain more responses that *conform* to the investigator's suggestions; and investigators who are warmer towards people tend to obtain more *pleasant* responses'. Quite recently it was found that people are more likely to sort photographs into emotionally positive categories with 'friendly' experimenters than they are when the same experimenters are 'neutral' in their manner (Hoffman *et al.*, 1970).

The morality of experiments in which subjects are 'tricked' is seriously being questioned. In experiments such as Milgram's the 'experimenters' were clearly put into what would be an emotionally disturbing situation and some were reported to be looking white and shaken when they had finished their work. Milgram says they were all told about the nature of the experiment afterwards and 'reassured', but possibly some were permanently affected by having seen themselves *able* to inflict pain on others. Kelman (1967) discusses and illustrates the moral problems which are inevitable aspects of psychological experimentation.

In his paper 'On the social psychology of the psychological experiment' Orne (1962) quoted the following passage from Pierce, written in 1908:

It is to the highest degree probable that the subject('s) . . . general attitude of mind is that of ready complacency and cheerful willingness to assist the investigator in every possible way by reporting to him those very things which he is most eager to find, and that the very questions of the experimenter . . . suggest the shade of reply expected. . . . Indeed . . . it seems too often as if the subject were now regarded as a stupid automaton. . . .

Orne describes how he asked some acquaintances to do the experimenter a favour by performing five press-ups and how they asked in amazement *why*? He asked another similar group of people to take part in a short experiment involving doing five press-ups and they asked simply *where*? There is a clearly defined social situation called 'taking part in an experiment' in which the specific 'roles of subject and experimenter are well understood and carry with them well-defined mutual role expectations'.

In a previous study (Orne, 1959) it was found that a particular experimental effect only occurred with those subjects who were able to state what the experimenter's hypothesis was.

. . . it is futile to imagine an experiment that could be created without demand characteristics. One of the basic characteristics of the human being is that he will ascribe purpose and meaning. In an experiment where he knows some purpose exists, it is inconceivable for him not to form cues, no matter how meagre; this will then determine the demand characteristics which will be perceived by and operate for a particular subject. Rather than eliminating this variable then, it becomes necessary to take demand characteristics into account, study their effects, and manipulate them if necessary (Orne, 1962).

Work indicating that the psychological experiment is a 'social situation' has been stressed because it underlines the importance of reflexivity in psychological theory. Construct theory sees the 'psychologist' and his 'subject' as being in the same interpretive boat and is designed to break us of the habit of playing at being 'scientists' in the ritual sense of the term.

When we talk about the subject understanding the experimenter's hypothesis, we are using Kelly's notion of *role*. This is stated within the sociality corollary: to the extent that one person construes the construction processes of another, he may play a role in a social process involving the other person. (Be it noted that playing a role in relation to another person does not necessarily mean agreeing with him.) Kelly goes on to state:

Here we have a take-off point for a social psychology. By attempting to place at the forefront of psychology the understanding of personal constructs, and by recognizing, as a corollary of our Fundamental Postulate, the subsuming of other people's construing efforts as the basis for social interaction, we have said that social psychology must be a psychology of interpersonal understandings, not merely a psychology of common understandings (Kelly, 1955, p. 95).

This position offers us a potentially unifying concept between individual and social psychology.

In an experiment designed to study the relationship between role construing and perceived similarity in behaviour it was found that if people A and B are construed by C as being similar, then C considered that he would behave similarly towards them (Bender, 1968). What was not shown is the extent to which C *would* actually behave more similarly towards A and B than to a third person who is differentially construed. Yet would one expect any other outcome, particularly as there is increasing evidence that one's construing of events determines one's behaviour, as indicated by Rosenthal, Orne and others (e.g. Marcia *et al.*, 1969; Fransella, 1971a; Marks and Gelder, 1967)?

Social psychology

In the traditional social psychology experiment we are presented with the study of interactions between subjects rather than between experimenter and subject. Investigation is made of the attitudes of subjects, not the attitudes of the experimenter. To indicate ways in which personal construct theory may throw new light on old issues, a few topics have been selected for discussion.

Conformity

In the now famous Asch experiments (1951), groups were made up of one genuine subject and several 'stooges'. They were given different tasks to do, but in a typical experiment they were asked to state which of the three lines in the comparison card in Figure 4 was the same as that in the standard card.

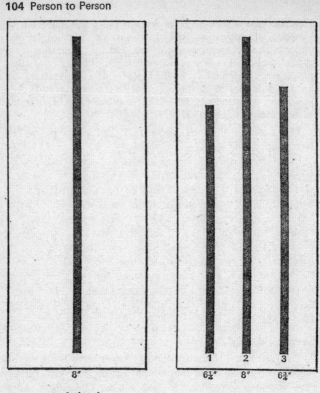

Figure 4 Standard and comparison cards used in a
group-pressure experiment
(From Asch, 1956)

In one of the trials designed to exert group pressure, the
majority of the stooges chose the six and a quarter inch line.
In the first experiment of this kind, 37 per cent of the 'real'
subjects agreed with the majority. Life does not often give us
such invalidatory experiences and so what is the poor
person to do? In subsequent interviews, most said they questioned their own judgement and not that of the majority; we

seldom expect to be the only sane being in the midst of a group of madmen (except, seemingly, in a psychological experiment). In the face of this overwhelming invalidating evidence, belief in our own judgement must be very strong indeed for us to hang on to it. Apparently even those who had the courage of their convictions felt very uncomfortable, one reporting that 'despite everything, there was a lurking fear that in some way I did not understand I might be wrong – a fear of exposing myself as inferior in some way'.

Construing the event as 'well, I never was much good at measures anyway' was one way the subjects dealt with invalidating evidence (a handy superordinate probably more readily resorted to by women than men). Another reaction was to show hostility, in the Kellian sense. For instance, one subject convinced himself that he was sitting in a position which gave him a different visual angle to the lines from the rest, which in turn gave him a distorted image. He was 'extorting validational evidence in favour of a type of social prediction which had already proved itself a failure'. It might well be fruitful to find out what led the subjects to respond in the way they did, both in terms of their own construing and in terms of construct theory notions dealing generally with reactions to invalidating evidence.

A considerable amount of work has been done on conformity both in investigating the sorts of situations likely to enforce it and seeking to identify the more or less conforming person – the trait of conformity. Bannister (1970c) has argued that trait theories are 'tautological in two senses – they inhibit the development of concepts of process and change and they produce unelaboratable concepts of original cause' (p. 412). In the case of conformity it would advance our knowledge more if we were to study the type of interactive construing likely to produce agreement or non-agreement between people. If a person construes himself as being independent of others, sets high store on forming his own opinions and does not believe that the majority usually knows best, then he is more likely to be nonconformist in *circumstances in which for him these constructs pertain*. If, on the other hand, he *either* does not consider agreement or disagreement among people important but stresses the need to sum up each situation on its own merits *or* if he believes that one of the most valuable things in life is to get with people, not upset them and so forth, then he will be more likely to go along with their ideas. Looking at individual construing systems in particular contexts will tell us more about agreement and disagreement than measuring people on some scale designed to place each at some point along a 'conformity' continuum.

Conforming behaviour in children was investigated by Salmon (1969). She did not seek some general characteristic of the child, but investigated the extent to which the attitude of the parents determined whether the child would be more likely to be influenced by other children or by adults. She concluded that:

the results also seem to support the view that conformity to particular social pressures is not an inborn characteristic of the subject, but is the outcome of his previous experience of crucial members of the relevant social groups. Boys who had experienced accepting rather than rejecting attitudes from their mothers tended to take *either* adults *or* peers as a reference group, rather than responding in an indiscriminate way to both.

Social class attitudes

In a stratified society each sub-group tends to have its own code of behaviour, manner of speaking and non-verbal forms of behaviour which serve to 'tell' strangers where each fits into the general social scene. Bernstein (1961) has suggested that in England there are also fundamental linguistic differences that influence how people psychologically organize their experiences; in other words, differences in how they construe. He follows Whorf (1956) in believing that the language we speak is an important determinant of how we think. Construct theory would certainly contend that there was a close relationship between construing and language but also contends that construing can take place at a non-verbal level – constructs are fundamentally discriminations which need not necessarily be verbalized.

Bernstein (1959) states that the middle and working classes in England speak virtually different languages, the former using an 'elaborated' linguistic code and the latter a 'restricted' one. Having described the characteristics of 'restricted' speech, he goes on to say:

If some of the characteristics are examined – short, grammatically simple, syntactically poor sentence construction; inappropriate verbal forms; simple and repetitive use of conjunctions; rigid and limited use of adjectives and adverbs; selection from a group of traditional phrases; the very means of communication do not permit, even discourage, individually differentiated cognitive and affective responses.

There is a vast difference in mother calling to child, 'Stop kicking that dog' and 'You must not be cruel to dumb animals'.

Bernstein is not talking so much about what is called intelligence but about a much wider issue; he is saying there is a whole way in which two groups may differ in how they organize their thought processes. Warren (1966) tried to put some of Bernstein's ideas to the test by giving repertory grids to thirty sixth-formers at a public school and to a group of day-release students at a technical college. They were selected so as to be homogeneous within each group for social class. He found that the middle-class boys related constructs in a more individualistic way, and comments that this was particularly striking since the public school boys were in fairly constant contact with each other, whereas the day-release boys met only once a week. One of the significant findings was unpredicted. One of the constructs used was *unusual,* and this was seen as something at the 'bad' end of the scale for the working class boys, whereas it was considered as an independent construct dimension for the middle class boys. The construct *unusual* is also evaluatively 'bad' for neurotics (Bannister, 1962a). Bannister argued that if neurotics were thought of as having simple, relatively inflexible construct systems, then anything unusual would be seen as threatening and therefore undesirable. Warren similarly concludes:

... as a result of their restricted code the working-class group have less adequately organized cognitive systems, and will therefore tend to see any 'unusual' element as something of a threat, since their construing systems are relatively less adequate for subsuming and predicting the behaviour of the 'unusual' element.

Wherever people with radically different construing processes view the same event, we can expect disagreement. In the world of international relations, when people who speak different *languages* find it hard to understand each other at the best of times, how important then must be the nationality of the interpreter who imposes his own construing system on what the protagonists are saying.

Non-verbal communication

A great deal of the research that has been carried out under this heading has been 'external' to the people involved. Argyle *et al*. (1970) say:

It is now familiar that human social interaction consists not only of verbal exchanges but also of non-verbal signals, such as head-nods, facial expression, gesture, posture, eye-movements, tones of voice. It is known that these non-verbal signals play a number of separate roles, including the communication of interpersonal attitudes, the expression of emotions, self-presentation, indicating mutual attentiveness, providing feedback, handling floor-apportionment, and providing illustrations for speech.

These studies are useful in classifying the sorts of signals people in this culture use to communicate with one another. However, it seems that gesture is being looked on as a more or less translatable equivalent for words, whereas it might be better viewed as the special index of kinds of non-verbal superordinate and loose construing. Argyle recognizes this broad point – 'the non-verbal code would lose its valuable property of vagueness whereby interactors are not committed to a particular relationship, and shifts in attitude can be made quite easily' (Argyle, 1969, p. 433).

Studies on non-verbal communication link with those on the 'experimenter effect' in that they are trying to isolate how expectancies, attitudes and so forth are communicated. In an early experiment (Kelley, 1950) students were given descriptions of a visiting lecturer. All students were given identical descriptions except for one item; half were told he was 'rather cold' and the others that he was 'very warm'. Having listened to him lecture, everyone rated him as intelligent, but the 'warm' students rated him as more considerate of others, better informed, more sociable, more popular, better natured, more humorous and more humane than did the 'cold' students. During the discussion period afterwards, 56 per cent of the 'warm' students participated in the discussion whereas only 32 per cent of the 'cold' group did so. Here again the effect can be explained as a function of the superordinate position of *warm-cold* in most people's repertoire of 'personality' constructs – thereby a multiplicity of subordinate constructs are implied. One of the interesting features of the Kelley experiment was that the differential construing of the lecturer led to differences in participation in communication with the lecturer, thereby illustrating the 'self-fulfilling prophecy' element of many of our acts of construing. We see X as 'cold', we treat X as 'cold' and we then find him truly 'cold'.

Cognitive complexity

A considerable amount of work carried out within the framework of personal construct theory has concentrated on a concept of 'cognitive complexity'. Bieri (1966) says that 'cognitive complexity may be defined as the tendency to construe social behaviour in a multidimensional way, such that a more cognitively complex individual has available a more versatile system for perceiving the behaviour of others than does a less cognitively complex person'. He argues that as a person develops socially so his ways of construing people become more complex; he has more ways or dimensions along which to describe what he perceives in others.

Adams-Webber (1969) extended Bieri's ideas and method of analysis to investigate the notion that 'relatively cognitively complex persons will exhibit more skill than relatively cognitively simple persons in inferring the personal constructs of others in social situations'. To test this, he elicited constructs from thirty people, each person showing how these were related *for him* in a repertory grid. A person who has a grid in which there is a high degree of matching between ticks is relatively cognitively simple, since he construed the people in the grid in similar ways; a person with low matching scores is relatively cognitively complex since he applied the constructs in different ways to the people in the grid. The cognitively simple person has a stereotyped view of people, seeing certain combinations of qualities as inevitably going together. These subjects were called together again three weeks later and paired. They were told to discuss a holiday they would like to go on together, money being no object. When they had done this, they were each given a list of forty-four bi-polar constructs, twenty-two of which were those that had been elicited from their partner. They had to identify the twenty-two constructs that came from their partner. As Adams-Webber had predicted, the more cognitively complex a person, the more accurate he was in identifying the constructs used by his partner; perhaps because he was better able to take in other people's ideas than subjects who had only a few dimensions at their disposal.

A variation of this score (McComsky *et al.*, 1969) has been used to show that architectural students who have many different ways of construing ideas about buildings do much better in examinations than others (Canter, 1970) and that this is *not* related to 'intelligence' as conventionally conceptualized and measured.

This further underlines the argument that describing construing as 'simple' or 'complex' is at best only meaningful in relation to sub-systems, not in relation to whole personal construct systems. There is, in fact, need for much caution here. It would be very easy to fall into the error of thinking of cognitive complexity-simplicity as a trait dimension on which a person occupies a fixed position. There is no reason to suppose any such thing. A person could well be extremely cognitively complex in relation to other people and yet simple when dealing with his family (or subtle when pondering paintings but crude on the topic of cats).

Aggression (the active elaboration of one's perceptual field) may occur when a person experiences anxiety. To some people social relations may be more anxiety-provoking than family situations, so one subsystem is elaborated and becomes 'complex' and not the other.

Within limits, a person may be particularly aggressive in the area of his anxiety. This is the area in which his constructs seem partially to fail to embrace the events at hand within their proper ranges of convenience. In his effort to explore the uncharted area, the person may set up a rapid succession of choices and select alternatives among them (Kelly, 1955, p. 509).

That this characteristic of construing can vary from situation to situation or from time to time does not mean it cannot be studied. More information about the process will help us understand more about people and their reactions. Thus our suspicion that neurotics have relatively simple interpersonal systems leads us to try and help them elaborate this subsystem, so enabling them to deal more readily with people's multiple quirks.

Prejudice

A potent source of social conflict and misery has been the resentment which minority groups of all kinds seem to arouse; in almost all cultures the 'out-group' is regarded with anxiety and hostility, treated as a threat. This reaction to others has frequently been termed 'prejudice' and a typical definition is that given by Krech, Crutchfield and Ballachey (1962) 'an unfavourable attitude towards an object which tends to be highly stereotyped, emotionally charged and not easily changed by contrary information'. If we review the kind of phenomena covered by the term prejudice, in construct theory terms, we can argue the immediate relevance of two major constructs from the theory.

Firstly, a 'prejudiced' argument seems to involve an extensive use of constellatory and pre-emptive constructs. The constellatory construct which 'fixes the other realm membership of its elements' is characteristic of stereotyped or typological thinking – the view that if a man is a Negro it necessarily follows that he must be *lazy, musical, highly sexed, low on washing* and *high on laughter*. But additionally and more dangerously the prejudiced argument seems to use its constellatory constructs in a pre-emptive manner. The pre-emptive mode of using constructs is one which claims the elements of the construct for membership in its own realm *exclusively*. Thus the view that if this man is a Negro he is *nothing but* a Negro; he is not simultaneously available to be viewed as a human being, a chess player or a brother-in-law.

The second characteristic of prejudiced thinking, in construct theory terms, arises from the linked notions of core constructs and hostility. It seems likely that for each of us our prejudiced ideas are core ideas, they involve dimensions along which we choose to see ourselves and others most significantly – they refer to maintenance processes. Thus, any invalidation of our expectations in terms of these constructs would imply the need for a major revision of our outlook, a revision for which we may be ill-prepared. If these core ideas are experienced as being less meaningful, then we are threatened, we are made aware of 'imminent comprehensive change in our structures' (Kelly), or 'imminent comprehensive reduction of the total number of predictive implications of our personal construct system' (Hinkle, 1965).

Our reaction to such potential chaos is almost inevitably *hostility*. We refuse to be wrong, we set out to extort validational evidence for our prejudices, we cook the books, we deny the validity of the source of contradictory evidence. The essence of prejudice is that we use our constructs in a given area in an entirely non-propositional way, there are no 'ifs' or 'buts'. We hold these constructs to be major dimensions for making sense out of central aspects of our life. Therefore, in order to safeguard our psychological stability or even our sanity we become hostile towards conflicting evidence.

To re-define such concepts as 'prejudice' in construct theory terms may look simply like playing the name-changing game. But it can be more than this. By talking in terms of constellatory constructs, core-role construing and so forth, we are bringing what was previously a relatively isolated area of study within a general framework so that it can be related to other 'psychology'. It may be possible thereby to relate it to our construing of psychological change.

By definition prejudice is an attitude (constellation of constructs) which is resistant to change. We have argued that the resistance stems from the fact that the implications of the constellation of constructs are too extensive for the person lightly to undertake change – too much is thereby entailed.

In the light of this argument consider, say, the study of Deutsch and Collins (1951) who were able to investigate change in degree of prejudice in a natural social experiment in America. They concentrated on two different types of housing estate – segregated and integrated. In the former there were different sections of the estate for Negroes and whites and in the latter allocation of houses was on the basis of first come, first served – no note of colour being made against the name of the applicant. It was thus possible to study the reduction of prejudice, if any, as a function of the degree to which 'prejudiced people are brought into situations that compel contact between them and the objects of prejudice'. These psychologists were arguing that such a situation would reduce prejudice providing that 'the intimacy and amount of contact with objects of prejudice not conforming to the stereotypes of the prejudiced are such as to result in experiences which are sufficiently compelling to resist marked perceptual and memorial distortion'. Leaving aside the mild air of tautology in this proviso, the experiment clearly showed that there had been a reduction in 'prejudice'. However, it also showed that the reduction was only a reduction and not complete elimination, and that for a number of people there had been no lessening in prejudice at all.

This suggests that simple experience *as such* may not be an effective agent of change – it does not of itself involve reconstruction. Kelly repeatedly pointed out that we can have ten experiences of an event if we reconstrue each time, or else have one experience *repeated* ten times if we fail to reconstrue. Prejudiced people, one suspects, are more familiar with the latter type of experience. It may be that the lessening of prejudice involves a change in the very way we construe, from constellatory and pre-emptive construing to propositional construing, largely without reference to particular objects of prejudice. By the strange economics of psychology it may be quicker and more effective to try and help a person to recast his construing strategies altogether, as a method of lessening prejudice, rather than directly trying to persuade him that Negroes, Jews, gypsies, homosexuals or Eskimos are really all right people.

Additionally, we might note that such is the ingenuity of man that he has more ways of limiting the implications of his own stereotypes than simply abandoning them. He can suspend elements from the range of convenience of constellations of constructs – sometimes on such a scale that the constellation is taken out of business. He finds endless 'exceptions to the rule'. There is evidence that individuals frequently make themselves an exception to stereotypical rules even where they accept the 'truth' of the general statement. Fransella (1968) found that not only do fluent speakers have a stereotype of a 'stutterer', but stutterers hold this same stereotype – yet make exceptions of themselves. They seem to be saying that others conform to this picture of the stutterer but 'I am different, I am unique, I stutter but I am not a stutterer'. A related finding, with further implications about ways in which we can modify and handle our stereotypes, is reported by Hudson. In his study of stereotypes about 'arts' and 'science' people he found that the former are rated (on a semantic differential) as *warm, imaginative* and *exciting* while the latter are seen as *dependable, valuable* and *intelligent*. However, boys who were classified as 'arts' or 'science' did not relate *themselves* to one or the other stereotype – they saw themselves as having the good qualities of both. Hudson then had the boys rate four different sorts of 'self': actual, ideal, perceived (who the teacher took them to be) and future (who they expected to be in ten years' time). The 'actual self' discriminated best for the artistic characteristics and the 'perceived self' for the scientific virtues. Hudson speculates as to whether this reflects a situation in which 'artistic virtues are perceived accurately by internal reference by looking inside oneself; while scientific virtues are perceived accurately by reference to the relations of others – and especially to figures of authority like the teacher' (Hudson, 1970, p. 74).

In our search for the ultimate psychological foundations of prejudice we might look, not to sophisticated versions of the 'herd instinct' idea or to the notion of unfortunate conditioning, but rather to our tendency to see our interpretations of the world as facts of the reality out there rather than interpretations. It may be that you have to be a naïve realist to have the confidence to hold a really vehement 'prejudice'.

Brain washing

In recent years a great deal has been talked about a radical experiment in changing men's construing systems, that of brain washing. This does not refer so much to the Russian variety, designed apparently to elicit specific confessions, but to the Chinese variety described by such people as Lifton (1961). Their aim, it seems, is not to extract confession of a 'crime' as such, but to undertake 'idealogical remoulding'. The methods used for such gigantic 'reconstruction' are worth noting.

Lifton describes one man who was suddenly arrested and

placed in a cell with eight other men, all more 'advanced' in their reform than he. They could only advance further by getting the newcomer to confess. Their attitude was one of basic certainty about the rightness of his arrest. No one was arrested unless known to be guilty, therefore why not confess now and save everybody time and trouble. After several hours the man was taken to the interrogation room where again protestations of innocence were ignored and the certainty of the prisoner's guilt stressed. After many hours of such questioning, the man was handcuffed and returned to the cell where the struggle with his cell-mates went on.

You are obliged to stand with chains on your ankles and holding your hands behind your back. They don't assist you because you are too reactionary. You eat as a dog does, with your mouth and teeth. You arrange the cup and bowl with your nose to try and absorb broth twice a day. If you have to make water they open your trousers and you make water in a little tin in the corner. ... In the W.C. someone opens your trousers and after you are finished they clean you. You are never out of the chains. Nobody pays any attention to your hygiene. Nobody washes you. In the room they say you are in chains only because you are a reactionary. They continuously tell you that, if you confess all, you will be treated better.

The savage echo of the Asch 'social conformity' experiments is apparent. In time, exhaustion may win, and the man start to 'confess' to anything. Then comes the re-education process – seeing things from the 'people's' viewpoint. With some prisoners this was apparently highly effective.

There have been many theories as to why people can be made to accept things they 'know' to be untrue and come to accept doctrines foreign to their basic beliefs. Particularly significant is the attack on the core construing – including that to do with being 'human'. To be made totally dependent on others; to have to behave like an animal and to be denied one's name (all prisoners were given numbers) invalidates aspects of superordinate construing. Add to this the physical rigours and sleep deprivation and it would be expected that 'loosening' of construct relationships would follow. Repeated invalidation of this sort leading to loosening, followed by the persistent offer of a total pre-packaged philosophy might well amount first to producing psychological chaos for the victim, followed by offering him salvation in a new 'structure'.

As a relevant anecdote it may be noted that we once repeatedly gave grids to a patient who had become the beneficiary or victim of simultaneous and competing treatments. She was given enthusiastic behaviour therapy by a psychologist, who tried to convince her that her symptoms had no personal significance and were merely maladaptive; learned habits which could be neatly cut away from her by re-training. Simultaneously, she was treated by an enthusiastic psychiatrist who strove to convince her that her symptoms related to deep personal problems and that removal was only feasible as part of a fairly major personality change. After nearly a year of these uncoordinated attentions, the grid showed that the inter-correlations between the patient's constructs had dropped virtually to zero, indicating a gross loosening of her construing. At the same time she complained of feeling unreal, of being totally given up to fantasies, of not knowing who she was. It was even noticeable that she repeatedly bumped into doorways and chairs and seemed hardly aware of the boundaries of her own body. It is possible that the patient had been, for practical purposes, 'brain washed', and was prime and ready for any indoctrination, Marxist, Christian or as per Samuel Smiles. As fate and the hospital decreed she was left alone at this point and appeared, by herself, gradualy to reinstate her original view of the world.

Returning to Lifton's account, how is it that some prisoners resisted remoulding and some could not? After three years, the man mentioned came to believe a considerable amount of what he confessed to, but says that: 'You begin to believe all this, *but it is a special kind of belief*. You are not absolutely convinced, but you accept it – in order to avoid trouble – because every time you don't agree, trouble starts again.'

Somewhere in his system, the person has to keep some construct relationships intact, particularly preserving the implications of superordinate constructs – e.g. 'I am saying all this to save my life'. Here the prisoner is taking a meta-view of his situation, he is construing his constructs. This man, on release, said he missed certain aspects of prison life and was confused and afraid. Brown (1963) points out that such feelings are common among prisoners and hospital patients who have been away from general social contact for a long time. Such institutionalization comes about largely because the inmates are viewed as objects rather than people – they lose their superordinate identity.

There is very little evidence about the relative resistance of individuals to psychological pressures of this extreme sort, but an intimate knowledge of a person's superordinate construct system should enable certain predictions to be made. A deeply religious belief in the support of a supernatural power has produced many martyrs. Koestler's novel *Darkness at Noon* implies that Russia has produced a system of superordinate construing that dictates that an individual should 'confess' to crimes against the State for the good of the State, the service thus provided to the State being more important than the 'technical' truth of the confession or the epitaph of the individual. These old guard Bolsheviks suffered a double martyrdom.

In Korea it seems that pro-rata many more American personnel were 'persuaded' to communist beliefs than either Turkish infantrymen or British officers (Shein, 1956). The 'brain washed' were found to comprise mainly those who had low intelligence, no previous foreign service, lower social class, poor integration with their military unit and no firm religious beliefs. This does not tell us much about their superordinate construing, but being poorly integrated with their unit may have been associated with poorly defined construing of personal identity. In both these respects they would be contrasted with the British officer and Turkish infantryman groups, in whom both identification with unit and country is very pronounced. It may be that efforts on the

Turkish infantrymen foundered because the persuaders were non-Muslim, non-members of the Turkish officer corps and thereby invalid as sources of 'evidence'; equally for British officers the Chinese interrogators were essentially construed as 'foreigners' so that their arguments were 'irrelevant'. Thus, Kellian 'hostility' saved the day. This general argument is that the more clearly the superordinate construing is elaborated the less chance there is of 'thought reform' being successful.

Groups

While Asch studied in the laboratory the effects of psychological pressure by a number of people on one person, others have studied what happens within groups. Probably the most 'non-personal' research of person interaction has been that of Leavitt (1951). He wanted to evaluate systems of communicating between five people and he allowed them to communicate with one another only by posting messages through holes in screens. For the solution of simple problems, it appeared quickest if subject X could exchange information with the other four, but the other four could only communicate through X. For complex problems, quicker solutions were reached if each person could pass notes to those on his left and right. Burgess (1968) has commented on the artificial nature of these experiments and shown how some of their conflicting results, over the past twenty years, are inevitable because of the artificiality of the situations.

However, using construct theory goggles, one would be unlikely to embark on such mechanical experiments. Nor would construct theory lead one to study group interaction by analysing the *quantity* of communication by each person. Borgatta and Bales (1953), for instance, counted the amount of communication between members of groups who had not met before and classified people into high, medium and low communicators. Groups were then reconstructed so that they contained either all high, all low, all medium or 'mixed' communicators. The highest rate of interaction and highest satisfaction was in the mixed group. This type of word counting may be of interest in itself, but again, construct theory would not ask such a question, unless perhaps word rates were to be related to people's views of each other and themselves.

More illustrative of a construct theory approach is a study (Triandis, 1959) using Kelly's elicitation method, in which the interaction between construing and effectiveness of communication was demonstrated. Triandis elicited constructs about jobs and about people from a large number of workers and supervisors in a factory. These constructs were then formed into semantic differential scales. The jobs rated on the 'job' semantic differential were: welder, teacher, personnel director, vice president and clerk. The people constructs rated on the 'people' semantic differential were: the personnel director of the company, your supervisor, the boss of your supervisor, the vice president of your division, a fellow at work whom you like, an effective manager you have known well and who is not the same as any of the men already rated. Supervisor and worker found it easy to communicate with each other when they produced *similar* constructs (talked the same language) about people. The effect was even more marked when their constructs about jobs *interrelated* in a similar way.

If we apply the theory more generally in an industrial context, we may follow the argument of Howard (1970). He argues that it is important to distinguish between the Kellian concepts of hostility and aggression in management.

When a man has placed a bet he cannot afford to lose on predictions which evidence keeps showing were quite invalid and he keeps on extorting evidence or claiming the predictions occurred when it should be obvious that they did not, that man is hostile. . . . When we find him in a position of considerable power in a firm, it is a serious matter both for him and that firm. His hostility tends to broaden its coverage and he becomes more and more incapable, despite frantic and clever efforts, of realistically validating some of his predictions.

The aggressive man on the other hand is one who has ideas and goes out and puts them into practice, no matter what the obstacles – aggression being the active elaboration of one's construct system. He is often *called* hostile, but he is vastly different from the hostile man just described and he is as desirable in business as the other is destructive. Howard points out that it is all too easy to categorize people according to how their behaviour affects us – thus hostility and aggression are often seen as the same because they are equally uncomfortable to live with. We are tempted to argue that a man *must* be hostile if his behaviour hurts us, workers *must* be motivated to strike because they 'hate' the bosses, or because they are being led by 'trouble-makers'. Perhaps if more people applied Kelly's first principle and went and asked the workers how they perceived their problem, they might be told. It must be remembered that 'asking' in construct theory terms is not of the simple question-and-answer kind, it means attempting to construe the construction processes of another in the hope that we will be able to 'see' the situation through his eyes.

A study concerned with group interaction in terms of construct theory and grid method (Fransella and Joyston-Bechal, 1971) demonstrated something resembling a 'group thought process'. Over twelve months, there was a fluctuation in the degree to which the constructs in each individual's grid were interrelated and the 'loosening' and 'tightening' was found to occur at similar times for most of the ten people. Of particular interest was the fact that a 'non-participating observer' also showed these 'sympathetic' fluctuations; it was as if he were swept along with the group (see Figure 5). In addition to the changes in intensity of construct relationships, there were changes in the degree of stability from one test to the next, with intensity changes *preceding* changes in stability; loosening occurred before people changed their ideas.

As the grids were the same for all members, and the elements used were the group members, it was possible to examine how well the 'group' agreed with an individual's view of himself. Each member ranked all the others, plus himself, on a number of constructs. If, for instance, person

A saw himself as being the leader of the group, one can look to see whether, in fact, all the other members ranked him first in terms of 'leadership'. A score of 'concordance of person perception' was worked out for each person by adding together the discrepancies between his view of himself and the group's view of him on all constructs. Among

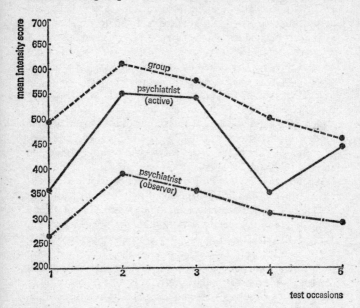

Figure 5 Variations in intensity of construing on five test occasions for a group of patients, a psychiatrist in charge of the group and a psychiatrist observing the group, over a period of twelve months
(From Fransella and Joyston-Bechal, 1971)

other things, it was found that some people were more accurate than others, with the two most accurate showing the most therapeutic improvement; there was greater accuracy on some constructs such as *leadership* and being *like the therapist* than on constructs such as being *disliked*.

Two kinds of change were demonstrated in this – change

in opinion about the members of the group or change in the implications of the constructs themselves. That is to say that persons A, B and C can be perceived as changing in terms of *leadership* qualities, but the qualities that define leadership remain the same. Alternatively, the *meaning* of leadership itself can change. It seems fairly likely that what often looks like change in opinion in discussion groups is no more than shuttling the elements to and fro along the construct dimensions, rather than active reconstruing or altering of the construct patterning.

This study was severely limited by the fact that only supplied constructs were used. It would no doubt be more profitable in future research to elicit some constructs so as to investigate the way in which person A's constructs may be picked up and used by persons B and C, and see how important for the group is the construing system of the person in charge of the group.

Directions

Kelly's suggestion that the notion of role could be a take-off point for a social psychology gives us not only new ways of tackling old problems but a way of unifying 'general' and 'social' psychology and abandoning them as separate 'psychologies'. That psychology must be stunted without integral concepts of 'sociality' is apparent. Leman (cf. 1970a) suggested that if we wanted to try and answer the curious question 'where is the mind', we might well say 'between people'. He was here stressing not simply our elaboration of ourselves through those we are directly involved with but our derivation from those who died long before we were born. The language we speak is our moulding of stuff we inherited – as are the constructs we use in our personal strategies: our mind is bequeathed to us, though we may give it a personal point and bequeath it as our own gift. Thus little of significance is likely to come forth from the psychologist who studies the 'isolated' functions of 'isolated' individuals. He cannot even draw a moral from the fact that his own style of experimental psychology was taught to him by a culture and he practises it as his continual interchange with that culture. But equally, without the construct of the individual person as the experiencing unit, social psychology becomes the delusion that 'society' is a unitary rule-bound mechanism whose nature can be uncovered by the concretistic strategies of epidemiology.

6 The Person in Need of Help

man the universal simp
follows lagging with a limp
treading on his neighbours toes
the way the little insect goes
in a million years or more
man may learn the simple lore
of how the bees are organized
and why the ants are civilized
may even hope for to approach
the culture of an average roach
if he is humble and not smug
may emulate the tumble bug

i look forward to the day
when the human race is done
and we insects romp and play
freely underneath the sun
and no roach paste is scattered
about anywhere i got another jolt of it
last night and today i seem to have a case
of intestinal flu the trouble with you
human beings is you are just plain wicked
                                        archy

DON MARQUIS, *archy's life of mehitabel,* 1931

For Kelly the focus of convenience of personal construct theory, however wide its range of convenience might be, was psychotherapy. It is not simply that he was personally a very involved, practising psychotherapist, but that he felt that two people struggling with major personal issues might prove a scientifically more rewarding focus for psychology than the navigational problems of the rat.

Any attempt by one person to be of psychological help to

another rests on some idea of the relationship between the two people. Formal approaches to psychotherapy all carry implications about this relationship. In psychoanalysis the relationship itself is a primary tool of the analyst – this is the meaning of 'transference' – but it seems to be overviewed as a case of 'doctor-patient'. Thus the analyst is the 'doctor', he comprehends the mysteries, he is the expert, he possesses the skill; the 'patient' is ill and hopes through the ministrations of the doctor to become well. True, the illness model, as used by psychoanalysts, offers explanations which are not available from the illness model used in orthodox psychiatry. In orthodox psychiatry the diagnostic labels (schizophrenic, depressive, anxiety state and so forth) are a mimic of diagnostic labels in general medicine and refer to crudely described behaviours, without offering any kind of process explanation of these behaviours. The analyst is armed with the psychodynamic explanation of the genesis of his patient. Client-centred psychotherapists adopt a stance which is reminiscent of that of an indulgent parent towards his child, while those following Ellis' rational emotive psychotherapy seem rather like authoritarian teachers in relation to their pupils.

Behaviour therapy

Behaviour therapists are only now making an explicit attempt to deal with the issue of the relationship between the two people involved in their therapeutic situation. On the one hand they refer to a segmented aspect of behaviour as a 'symptom' – which implies a use of the illness model – but they seem to have moved from 'doctor-patient' towards 'experimenter-subject'.

Behaviour therapy (Wolpe, 1954) is in many ways in contrast to most current methods for helping people with problems. It argues that symptoms are learned maladaptive habits rather than the result of some underlying conflict. Since they are learned, they could be unlearned, e.g. in the case of phobias, by substituting an emotion of pleasure for one of fear or anxiety. Wolpe put it more formally as: '. . . when fundamental psychotherapeutic effects are obtained in neuroses – no matter by what therapist – these effects are nearly always really a consequence of the occurrence of reciprocal inhibition of neurotic anxiety, i.e. the complete or partial suppression of the anxiety responses as a consequence of the simultaneous evocation of other responses psychologically antagonistic to anxiety . . .' (p. 205).

This reciprocal inhibition is attempted by constructing hierarchies of feared situations ranging from one that produces virtually no fear to one that brings on sheer panic and then presenting these to the phobic person, a step at a time. He gets used to each situation either by being put into it, e.g. by having a snake in a box at the end of the room, or else is made to relax deeply and then to imagine the situation.

For a long time the part played by the therapist was ignored and the person was considered to develop a love of snakes (for instance) because of the deconditioning process. But psychologists like Orne (1959) and Rosenthal and Jacobson (1966) and Rosenthal *et al.* (1966a) made it increasingly difficult for anyone to ignore the fact that people have expectations, even in conditioning procedures. The evidence that the expectation of the patient is related to 'symptom' improvement is mounting (e.g. Friedman, 1966 and Marcia, Rubin and Efran, 1969). The expectations of the therapist no doubt have their effects as well, but somewhat less is known about this.

Some people have translated these factors into operant conditioning terms; 'praise' or positive reinforcement is recommended as a deliberate addition to the deconditioning programme. Oliveau *et al.* (1969) compared the relative effectiveness of 'instructions' and 'praise' on the deconditioning of snake phobias. All groups improved, but those receiving therapeutic instruction improved more than the rest. The authors express some surprise that no effect was produced by praise. It may have been praise as construed by the therapist but perhaps the patient considered praise as irrelevant since he had been told the procedure had been found effective and that his fear of snakes would probably be reduced. A follow-up study showed that the improvement in those who had received therapeutic instructions had been maintained (Oliveau, 1969). The problem for the learning theorist is how to explain expectations in learning theory terms since it can no longer be considered part of the 'error variance'.

Kelly has this to say about behaviour therapy:

Now what about 'behaviour therapy', which is supposed to be at odds with humanistic psychology, and precisely so because it is 'rigorously scientific'? To my mind the only thing wrong with the accounts of behaviour therapy I have read is that they fail to mention who the principal investigator was. They call him a 'subject', while the fellow with the doctoral degree, who turns out to be only the technician in the project, is given credit for doing the experiment ...

Take, for example, the reverse snake charming experiment, which has become the popular prototype for behaviour therapy. The task is for a person who shudders at the sight of snakes to come to appreciate how very charming a snake can be. The first step is to entertain the hypothesis; although, like any proper hypothesis, it may not appear to be very realistic – at least not for the person engaged in the undertaking. The next step is to make a behavioural investment, that is to say, to pose the question behaviourally. That may not be what a philosopher would do, but it is what a scientist, who always doubts uncommitted rationality, must do. So the part to be played is the part of the scientist.

But a man making up to snakes may find himself floundering about in a multivariant predicament ... one may find, in the presence of too many snakes, that his behaviour has lost its composed directionality. If the old boundaries of safety are to be transcended in his approach to snakes and there is to be a conclusion to the experiment, new boundaries must be established *ad hoc*. In research language this means that each successive experiment must be 'controlled' if the research is not to become lost in a sea of 'variables'. Moreover, the specific hypotheses in each sequential inquiry must be clearly defined, else the principal researcher will not be able to determine what is confirmed by what.

And there is one final ingredient in the science of being charmed by snakes. The scientist – I'm still talking about the fellow who is trying out a new slant on snakes – must be left free at the conclusion of each step to decide just what experiment is to come next. Here, as elsewhere, the outcomes of scientific endeavours are often best judged by what the scientist, after searching his own reactions to his completed undertakings, decides to do next. It is preposterous to assume that the mere overt outcomes of one experiment make the scientist's next venture a cut and dried affair.

Now let us notice how the Wolpe type of behaviour therapy artfully contrives a procedure to enable the patient to become his own experimenter. Preliminary interviewing focuses attention on the general hypothesis that he can learn to live with snakes. It is, of course, only a hypothesis and therefore a ventured departure from the reality of the patient's world. The criteria against which accurate predictions will be assessed are defined in terms of the state of relaxation the patient may experience. He then practices relaxation so he will recognize it when he sees it.

Next the patient's fear is calibrated and a useful scale of aversion is constructed out of a graduated series of pictures of snakes, or actual distances measured from the snake itself. Experimental controls are established as *ad hoc* boundaries which can be successively moved out as the patient becomes bolder. Fantasy, or make-believe, is employed as the patient imagines his approach to the snake before he actually attempts it. . . . The patient is not pushed beyond the limits established for the current phase of his inquiry. Before each successive venture he must decide where the guard rails are to be placed, and he is free to return to their protective enclosure whenever he is threatened with incoherence. He does not surrender his initiative to another investigator. He observes carefully what happens – how frightened he is, or, rather, how relaxed he is, relaxation being operationally a better defined criterion for him than fright – and he notes how differently the snake appears as he approaches it. Finally, it is the patient, now a scientist planning his own actions, who decides what the next step in the experimental series will be. In this kind of therapy, behaviour is so clearly an experiment (Kelly, 1970b, p. 267).

As a more summary comment on the pure culture behaviour therapy approach Kelly (1965) once pointed out that psychiatry has a name for those who ignore the views and outlook of others, who seek only to manipulate their behaviour – they are called 'psychopaths'.

Construct theory psychotherapy

In construct theory psychotherapy the model for the relationship between the so-called therapist and the so-called patient is somewhat that of research supervisor to research student. Thus, just as a research student is in one sense more expert in his research field than his supervisor (since this field is chosen by him and he is totally committed to it, whereas it is only a part of the supervisor's interest), so the patient is the only informed expert on the situation in which he is personally involved. The research supervisor is an expert only in the sense that he is more conversant with research methods, more a veteran of past mistakes, than the student. Similarly the psychotherapist is more familiar with the ways in which people can entangle themselves and this is the wisdom which he has to offer. This research supervisor-research student model also has implications for the relationship between 'behaviour' and 'talk' and the relationship between the psychotherapy sessions and the client's life in the outside world. The client, like the research student, uses the sessions with his supervisor-therapist critically to discuss his theories about life, to examine the results of his past behaviour, to formulate hypotheses, to make tentative trial runs within the safe bounds of the psychotherapy session. In the periods between pschotherapy sessions he is an independent experimenter who puts his hypotheses to the test, gathers new data, unearths new confusions and takes back all this to the next session for joint critical review.

Approaches in psychotherapy have the additional problems of defining 'what is wrong' with the client and thereby selecting terms in which 'wrongness' is to be specified. If we are not going to view the client as 'ill' or suffering from 'a maladaptive learned habit' or having 'failed to actualize himself', then what terms do we use? We can follow the scientist model through and see the client as someone who is unable decisively to test out and elaborate his personal theories, his understanding of himself and his interpersonal world. His construing may have become circular, so that he is endlessly testing and retesting the same hypotheses and is unable to accept the implications of the data which he collects. He may have moved into the kind of chaos where his constructions are so vague and loose that they cannot provide him with expectations clear enough to be tested and they simply flow back and forth around the same issues. Whatever the specific difficulty, the psychotherapist is not setting out to sell his construct system to the client: he is trying to help the client to test the validity of the client's *own* construct system. If he is successful, in that the system once again begins to move and elaborate, then the direction in which it goes and the issues which it pursues are, in a very definite sense, no longer the psychotherapist's business.

Kelly outlined the therapist-client situation thus:

We have ruled out the notion of psychotherapy as the confrontation of the client with stark reality, whether it is put to him in the form of dogma, natural science, or the surges of his own feelings. Instead, we see him approaching reality in the same ways that all of us have to approach it if we are to get anywhere. The methods range all the way from those of the artist to those of the scientist. Like them both and all the people in between, the client needs to assume that something can be created that is not already known or is not already there.

In this undertaking the fortunate client has a partner, the psychotherapist. But the psychotherapist does not know the final answer either – so they face the problem together. Under the circumstances there is nothing for them to do except for both to inquire and both to risk occasional mistakes. So that it can be a genuinely co-operative effort, each must try to understand what the other is proposing and each must do what he can to help the other understand what he himself is ready to try next. They formulate their hypotheses jointly. They even experiment jointly and upon each other. Together they take stock of outcomes and revise their common hunches. Neither is the boss, nor are they merely well-bred neighbors who keep their distance from unpleasant affairs. It is, as far as they are able to make it so, a partnership.

The psychotherapy room is a protected laboratory where hypotheses can be formulated, test-tube sized experiments can be performed, field trials planned, and outcomes evaluated. Among other things, the interview can be regarded as itself an experiment in behaviour. The client says things to see what will happen. So does the therapist. Then they ask themselves and each other if the outcomes confirmed their expectations.

Often a beginning therapist finds it helpful to close his cerebral dictionary and listen primarily to the subcortical sounds and themes that run through his client's talk. Stop wondering what the words literally mean. Try to recall, instead, what it is they sound like. Disregard content for the moment; attend to theme. Remember that a client can abruptly change content – thus throwing a literal-minded therapist completely off the scent – but he rarely changes the theme so easily. Or think of these vocal sounds, not as words, but as preverbal outcries, impulsive sound gestures, stylized oral grimaces, or hopelessly mumbled questions.

But at other times the therapist will bend every effort to help the client find a word, the precise word, for a newly emerged idea. Such an exact labeling of elusive thoughts is, at the proper time, crucial to making further inquiries and to the experimental testing of hypotheses. Particularly is this true when the team – client and therapist – is elaborating personal constructs (Kelly, 1969, p. 228).

Looked at from the standpoint of personal construct theory, many current 'psychotherapies' are better viewed as isolated *techniques* rather than as total approaches in their own right. Thus a construct theory psychotherapy might well include behaviour therapy methods if the patient was having difficulty in tightening his construing in a given area. It might include a psychoanalytic type of free association if the patient had difficulty in loosening his constructs. But the construct theory psychotherapist would retain throughout the view that the client is essentially an experimental scientist in his own right, rather than someone to be manipulated by the behaviour therapist or absolved by the analyst.

Fixed role therapy

As one particular technique to be used with some clients, Kelly formulated the idea of fixed role therapy. It is in no way a panacea – rather it is a moderately useful technique when the psychotherapy has become circular and some trigger for movement is required. But it embodies and illustrates many of the ideals of construct theory psychotherapy.

The therapist who has decided to use fixed role therapy with a client first asks him to write a self-characterization. The client describes himself in the third person (beginning 'John Brown is . . .') from the viewpoint of a sympathetic friend. The psychotherapist examines this self-portrait and (usually in collaboration with another psychologist) draws up a *fixed role sketch* which is a portrait of a person who is psychologically at ninety degrees to the self-characterization of the client. The client is going to be asked to play the person described in this fixed role sketch and therefore should not be presented with a portrait of someone who is his diametric opposite. It is very difficult and threatening to enact an exactly opposite person and, in any case, the primary problem in development is to find new dimensions along which to see one's life, not to slot-rattle to the other end of dimensions which are already far too fixed. Thus, the fixed role sketch is not the opposite of the client, it is something that would involve the client in new but not over-demanding ventures.

This fixed role sketch is shown to the client and he is asked if he finds such a person credible. If he does not, the fixed role sketch is altered until he does. Next he is asked if he would find such a person broadly likeable. If he does not, the fixed role sketch is altered until he does. The client is then told that for a brief period (say three weeks) he is going to be the person in the fixed role sketch. The client is to eat the kind of food he thinks this person would eat, read the books he would read, respond to other people in the way in which this person would respond, dream the dreams this person would dream, and try to interpret his experience in terms entirely of this 'person'. It should be made clear to the client that this is a limited venture and that after a fixed period it will come to an end and he will revert 'to being himself'. It must be made clear that the fixed role is in no sense being set up as an ideal, it is merely a hypothesis for him to experiment with, a possibility for him to experience. During the short period of fixed role enactment the client sees the therapist frequently to discuss the interpretation of the fixed role, to consider the kind of experience he is getting, to play the role with the therapist.

At the end of the fixed role enactment it is hoped that the client will have experienced behaviours from people of a kind not likely to have been elicited by his usual 'self'. He will have been forced into a detailed psychological examination of this imaginary person and thereby have been less centred on himself. Above all, he may have begun to suspect that man is self-inventing and that he is not necessarily trapped forever inside his own autobiography and inside his own customary thought and behaviour.

Details of the technique of fixed role therapy are available in Kelly (1955), Bonarius (1970) and Karst and Trexler (1970). The point of stressing it in this context is to illustrate the emphasis on personal exploration and experiment which is the essence of construct theory psychotherapy.

The stutterer

An example of the application of the theory to explain a phenomenon and on the basis of this to plan a programme of 'treatment' is work on stuttering (Fransella, 1969; 1970a; 1971a; 1971b). Man is, psychologically, nothing but a bundle of constructs, or so says Kelly (being pre-emptive for emphasis). This being the case, then people must stutter because they view their world in some particular way. Stuttering could, of course, be viewed as a neurological abnormality, an anatomical defect or a personality disorder, but in a review of the literature (Beech and Fransella, 1968) the conclusion was reached that there was little evidence to suggest that any of these ways of viewing stuttering profited us much. In any case let the neurologists look for neurological defects, anatomists or surgeons look for anatomical defects and psychologists construe in psychological terms.

Man's aim, from a construct theory viewpoint, is to make the world as meaningful a place as possible. The more meaningful one way of behaving becomes as opposed to its alternatives, the more difficult it will be to change that behaviour. One can think of the lifelong stutterer as being a person who has built up a very elaborate subsystem of constructs to do with being a 'stutterer' and only sketchily construes being a fluent speaker – he has had little opportunity of experimenting as a fluent speaker. He therefore cannot readily change from stuttering to fluency – no one voluntarily walks the plank into the unknown depths of the ocean. Would there not be conceptual chaos if you were told that tomorrow you had to go out into the world as a member of the opposite sex? Your behaviour to men and women would have to be radically changed; how many gestures, mannerisms, ways of talking or walking or sitting would be misconstrued? Such a radical change would arouse extreme anxiety in the majority of people because of '*the awareness of the relative absence of implications with respect to the constructs with which one is confronted*'. Imagine also the threat in that situation because of '*the awareness of an imminent comprehensive reduction of the total number of predictive implications of the personal construct system*' (Hinkle, 1965).

Here, then, is a personal construct theory explanation of stuttering – that a person stutters because it is from this stance that the world is most meaningful to him. Before he can become a fluent person, this 'state of fluency' would have to be made more meaningful to him.

In a study of twenty stutterers, this was achieved by concentrating on the construing of fluency. The vast majority of stutterers, no matter how severe their disability, have moments of fluency. It was these that formed the basis of construct change and elaboration. Each fluent episode was discussed in great detail – *the stutterer was made to construe it* – everything about it. Only too often one finds that the stutterer has not done this when fluent. He has construed it globally as 'I was not stuttering'. He had not looked to see what difference this made to how he felt and behaved, how the listener reacted and what aspects of the situation might have led to his being fluent. The focus is on the *joint* search for common denominators in such situations.

To guide the self-exploration process and to give some quantitative data for comparison with changes in disfluencies, Impgrids were used. To monitor the relative meaningfulness of being a stutterer as opposed to being a fluent speaker, two such grids were repeated over time for each stutterer. For the 'stutterer' (S) grids, constructs were elicited by presenting triads consisting of two photographs of people and a card on which was written '*the sort of person people see me as being when I am stuttering*'. The same procedure was followed for the 'non-stutterer' (NS) grids, except that the card read *the sort of person people see me as being when I am NOT stuttering*'. These elicited constructs were then laddered (see Chapter 3 and Figure 3). Figure 6 shows how the total number of these implications changed over time with changes in disfluency. By termination of treatment thirteen out of seventeen had reduced their disfluencies by more than half, seven of these by more than 80 per cent.

Each stutterer wrote a self-characterization at the time of doing the Impgrids and having speech recordings made. These often gave quite different information from that elicited by the triadic method, partly because the Impgrids were concerned with the stutterer's view of himself in the speaking situation while the self-characterization was concerned with his global construing of himself *as a person*. The change that can be brought about in a person's view of the world can be seen in the following extracts from two self-characterizations by the same person.

At start of treatment programme

X is basically a worrier, which produces the attitude that things that go too well can't last. He is a serious person who was rather shy and something of an introvert in his youth. Today, however,

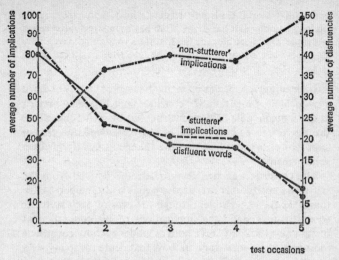

Figure 6 Changes in 'stutterer' and 'non-stutterer' implications and speech disfluencies on five test occasions during construct theory treatment of stuttering (From Fransella, 1971)

he has removed many evils of those attitudes.

He worries constantly about the impression he gives other people and tries to please and be popular in all forms of social intercourse. He has a very warm and human personality and although he regrets not having had a good education he has, through his own efforts largely, educated himself. His stammer has prevented him from allowing his personality to develop to the full as a non-stammerer's would be able to, and he feels unequal in an equal world.

Lastly, his happily married life has given him a necessary sense of responsibility for his family, from which stems the respect and love he seeks.

Eighteen months later

Today, X is a confident, self-sufficient person who through his own strong determination plus sympathetic external help has become a useful member of society.

He is now perfectly capable of taking his place in this tough competitive world. He is now leading a busy, active life and his lifelong stammer that has dogged him has been largely overcome.

People who meet him for the first time would find him mildly aggressive but always prepared to be interested in others' problems. Lastly, he will not suffer fools gladly.

Interestingly, X begins by seeing himself at the *shy* end of a *shy–sociable* dimension. He concludes not by seeing himself at the *sociable* pole of the construct but by seeing himself at the *aggressive* end of a new *aggressive–submissive* dimension. Note also that he views the change as largely his own achievement.

The constructs elicited from triads and derived from the self-characterizations are used to enable the helper to see things, as far as possible, through the eyes of each stutterer so as to understand the implications of his construing of fluent episodes. They serve both as guides to those constructs most easy to elaborate and to those that could resist any such change.

One unpredicted finding was that as one system became more meaningful (NS) so the other (S) became less so (see Figure 6). As one set of constructs is elaborated and validated so the other set is invalidated. We might wonder how far disuse is the functional equivalent of invalidation.

Fransella suggests that this concentration on the *construing* of fluency situations is the common denominator in successfully treated cases. Stutterers improve and remain improved if they are able to take advantage of instances of fluency by actively construing them. Others have the same fluent episodes but do not *experience* fluency.

In a comparison of this method with that of desensitization she stated that:

... at each stage the stutterer's capacity to construe and predict the situation is elaborated and his expectation of fear is invalidated. Successive invalidation of old constructs and elaboration of new inevitably change the nature of situations as they are perceived by the subject. Furthermore, it is held that placing a person in a specific situation will only lead to change in behaviour if he is made to reconstrue it (Fransella, 1969, p. 172).

She also speculates as to whether the same basic theory could not be applied to other life-long problems such as tics and phobias. People are unlikely to 'give up' something that is an integral part of themselves unless they become aware of the personally meaningful implications of the alternative ('desired') piece of behaviour.

The smoker

Mair (1970c) has suggested that it would be profitable to look at how the smoker construes himself in relation to his habit. It is all too generally assumed that people smoke 'from habit' and that therefore they can give it up if they did but try hard. But only a brief talk to smokers will reveal the complexity of this so-called habit. Smoking 'means' something to everyone, whether smoker or non-smoker. Progress might be made if the meaning for each individual person could be discovered. As with the stutterer and possibly the ticqueur, it is important also to discover the meaning of being a *non*-stutterer-ticqueur-smoker. If smoking is seen as *masculine, calming to the nerves* or enables one to give the appearance of *being confident* among strangers then to give up smoking might mean being seen as *unmasculine* or *jittery* or *ill at ease*. While not denying there is a drug effect, this should be seen in relation to the personal significance the effect has for each individual, the part that smoking plays has in his psychological economy.

The suicidal person

With the abandonment of the medical model, the most obvious alternative framework within which to construe people is that of 'personal interaction'. Just as Adler considered suicide to be the result of lack of social involvement (a disharmony between the social world and the individual) so Kelly constantly emphasizes the social implications of individual man's behaviour. He sees suicide 'as an act to validate one's life'. There are two occasions when the construction a person places on life may convince him that the abandonment of life is sensible.

The first is when the course of events seems so obvious that there is no point in waiting around for the outcome. The score has become so lop-sided, there is no reason to stay through to the end of the game. The other is when everything seems so utterly unpredictable that the only definite thing one can do is abandon the scene altogether. It has ceased to be a game with perceptible rules (Kelly, 1961b, p. 260).

Landfield (1971) takes up this latter explanation of suicide – that it is a desperate act to prove that there is some certainty in life, even if it is death. He builds his hypothesis concerning the instigating context of the suicidal attempt on Kelly's organization and choice corollaries. Commenting on the organization corollary Kelly says:

Different constructs sometimes lead to incompatible predictions, as everyone who has experienced personal conflict is painfully aware. Man, therefore, finds it necessary to develop ways of anticipating events which transcend contradictions (Kelly, 1955, p. 56).

Commenting on the choice corollary, Kelly states:

The principle of elaborative choice also includes a person's tendency to move towards that which appears to make his system more explicit and clear cut ... this may, in some instances, appear to call for constriction of one's field – even to the point of ultimate constriction, suicide (Kelly, 1955, p. 56).

When a particular effort at organization fails, constriction may occur in an attempt to retain some meaning. Instead of looking outwards around him so as to make sense of more and more of the world, he starts to look inward to limit his experiences and to define and restrict his construct system.

Landfield's hypothesis, based upon these two corollaries, is that suicidal behaviour will be found in the context of the disorganization and constriction of the person's construct system. Restated, 'suicidal behaviour will occur in the context of a decreasing ability to make sense of, interpret or react to one's personal world, most importantly, a personal world of people'. He derived measures from a form of Rep Test and gave the test to six groups of students, one group consisting of five students who had just made serious suicide attempts. Using a combined score on the three measures, the severe suicidal group had significantly higher average scores than the others. But Landfield points out, however, that ideally one wants to predict not post-dict.

According to construct theory, suicidal gestures or serious attempts necessarily produce evidence that the individual has then to incorporate into his system. What was it he validated or invalidated by finding himself conscious again when his last thoughts were of death? The act may produce enough of the evidence he sought to enable him to grasp at some organization and glance outwards again, if only in a tentative fashion. How difficult it is then to obtain predictive understanding by studying those who have *made* the suicidal attempt.

When faced with threat, guilt or an increasingly meaningless world, a person may react with hostility (making events fit predictions rather than predictions fit events). A person who has acted in this way for a long time, *making* the world around him fit how he thinks it must be, may well face conceptual disintegration if he is inescapably confronted with the fact that he has been wrong all along; if no new way of construing these events is offered to him, his whole system, including his core construing, may fall apart and he may commit suicide.

Lester (1968 and 1969) suggests that the suicidal person may be seeking to validate his opinion of the world as an unfriendly and unjust place as well as his opinion of his own worthlessness. In his later study, he found that suicidal individuals not only had fewer people to turn to in a crisis, but were more often dependent upon those they *resented*. Lester does not attempt to link up these findings to the notion of hostility. This would be possible if it were found that the person saw those on whom he was dependent as resenting *him,* and was trying to extort validational evidence that this was the case – 'by killing myself I prove that they wish me dead'.

The self

If we think of people not as belonging to illness categories but as individuals who have problems, then we are irrevocably led to the position of asking people what their trouble is. We can then try to understand their way of viewing the world so that we can help them to work out an alternative way of relating to others and their environment.

An example of this 'introspective' (Rychlak, 1968) attempt to deal with personal problems is given by Wright (1970). In his paper 'Exploring the uniqueness of common complaints', he says:

A symptom may be regarded as a part of a person's experience of himself which he has singled out and circumscribed as in some way incongruous with the rest of his experience of himself. It is normally something experienced as issuing from his *person*, but incongrous with his *view of himself* ('his self'). On account of the incongruity with the 'self', it tends to be regarded as *non-self* and is offered by the person as that which requires treatment (removal). . . .

Wright goes on to say that there are two approaches the therapist can make to the sufferer; he can fix him into some 'illness' or maladaptive response framework or he can explore with him what it is in his construing that has led to his present impasse. The former approach exploits the person's conviction that part of his behaviour is alien to him by encapsulating the problem in the medical model. Wright's study offers an excellent account of the 'reconstruction' approach in action for a particular person.

There have been other instances of this kind of *self–non-self* distinction. Figure 7 shows how an arsonist divorced himself (conceptually) from those who are likely to commit arson. Committing arson is not always regarded as a symptom of something, but it is well recognized as an anti-social act. Yet the arsonist seems to be saying that he, as a person,

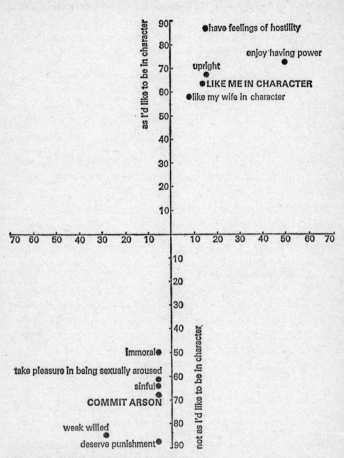

Figure 7 Relationship scores plotted along two axes for supplied and elicited constructs used by an arsonist.
(From Fransella and Adams, 1966)

is morally good, and that people who commit arson are morally bad. The authors suggest that this may often be the case when society says a person has comitted an anti-social act or suffers from an illness, and the person concerned sees himself as doing or meaning something quite different (Fransella and Adams, 1966).

Another example can be seen in Figure 8 (Fransella,

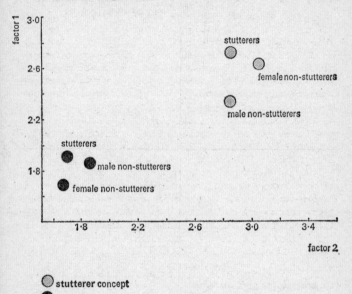

Figure 8 Constructs 'me' and 'stutterers' plotted along two dimensions of 'semantic space' for a group of stutterers, a group of male and a group of female non-stutterers (From Fransella, 1968)

1968). Here, groups of male and female non-stutterers and male stutterers completed semantic differential ratings of, among other things, the concepts *Me* and *Stutterers*.

The concepts occupy very different positions in the semantic space (they are given different meanings) *even for the stutterers*. Thus the stutterer seems to take the same view of other stutterers that non-stutterers take, but this is not the way he sees *himself*.

Construct theory differs from personality theories centred on the 'self' in that the self is seen as a construct along with all other constructs, albeit a very important construct. Kelly introduces the idea of self like this:

Let us turn our attention, more particularly, to the controlling effect one's constructs have upon himself. As we have pointed out before, the *self* is, considered in the appropriate context, a proper concept or construct. It refers to a group of events which are alike in a certain way and, in that same way, necessarily different from other events. The way in which the events are alike is the self. That also makes the self an individual, differentiated from other individuals. The self, having been thus conceptualized, can now be used as a thing, a datum, or an item in the context of a superordinate construct. . . .

When the person begins to use himself as a datum in forming constructs, exciting things begin to happen. He finds that the constructs he forms operate as rigorous controls upon his behaviour. His behaviour in relation to other people is particularly affected. Perhaps it would be better to say that his behaviour *in comparison* with other people is particularly affected. It is, of course, the comparison *he* sees or construes which affects his behaviour. Thus, much of his social life is controlled by the comparisons he has come to see between himself and others (Kelly, 1955, p. 131).

In 1965, Kelly wrote in a letter the following further notions about the self:

Now as for self-concepts: . . . I suppose I could start out with the sage comment that it should be called a self-percept rather than a self-concept. But I'm not sure I concur. The self may have the character of a construct as well as that of a construed event or object.

Assuming the self I am talking about when I refer to myself as an object, I am led to look for the dimensions in terms of which I suspend myself in psychological hyperspace. The more I follow this line of thought the more identity I have, the more static I feel and the more isolated I feel hanging over there all by myself. I'm not sure I like the idea. Identifying oneself in terms of his construct system can have this effect of making him feel immobilized, particularly if he uses constructs designed to take care of individual differences.

Of course I do want to be different from others – I think. But the implication is that I dare not change lest I slip into someone else's shoes. But suppose I used constructs that opened up for me channels of movement. Now what? Does this mean that I have relinquished my identity – my fixed identity – in order to live and be different from myself? I think so. But now, what is my 'self'? Is it an object fixed in space, or is it not the system of pathways I have opened up to movement? If it is the latter it is nearer to being a concept, or system of concepts, than it is to being an object to be perceived. Perhaps the self-concept is not a concept about the self but rather the set of concepts perpetrated by the self. How's that for confusing the issue?

Perhaps, as Kelly suggested at the beginning, there is the *self-as-a-construct* as distinct from the *self-as-an-element* which has an allotted place along other construct dimensions. This self-as-construct could be that intuitive 'me-ness' or consciousness, that permeates all our life. The self-as-element is a series of specific distinctions which we make between ourselves and others in particular contexts – this self is a datum which sits somewhere along many dimensions. The operational distinction between the two is explored by Mair (1967).

Perhaps in *derealization* the self as construct is alienated from its elements, retaining only awareness, and so is able to 'watch' the self *as if it were* an object, performing its own acts in terms of its own discriminations. It seems that the majority of people stand back and 'watch' themselves from time to time, but retain the capacity to refocus on elements so that awareness is again associated with acts. A familiar experience of derealization occurs when we are intoxicated or feverish. We feel as if the world is separated from us; we are watching ourselves perform actions that do not belong to us or seem to be our responsibility; we watch ourselves having a conversation with someone and comment to ourselves about the role we are playing. Drug-taking appears to accentuate this self-as-construct – self-as-element dichotomy.

There have been reports of people being able to withstand torture by making themselves view their bodies as objects for which they had no reponsibility and this 'view' is often suggested to surgical patients when hypnosis is the anaesthetic agent.

Depersonalization can be viewed as the reverse of de= realization in that the person feels that he is unreal although the world is real enough. It may be a state in which the person's subordinate grasp of concrete and detailed reality is intact but his superordinate 'me' has weakened – he cannot draw together the strands of personal detail into a sub- suming 'I'.

That there is something other than the self-as-element sit- ting along numerous continua, is suggested by the fact that we do not always see imitation as being the sincerest form of flattery. To be told that one of our students is clearly using 'our style' is supposed to please, perhaps it does, until we see that person in operation. To see too much of oneself mir- rored can be a threat to consciousness of our 'uniqueness'. The same thing applies if we are told that our style of writ- ing is very similar to another's or that we have a double.

What happens to personal uniqueness if one is a twin? Twins sometimes seem to make a concerted effort *not* to be unique. But on reflection, it appears that they are delib- erately *playing the role* of being indistinguishable. They behave as 'identical' because society believes they will be. It is a conspiracy between them. They are aware that, in fact, they are very different.

If there are these two types of self, then the one that is being measured in repertory grids or other techniques is not the 'uniqueness' aspect of self but some variant of the self- as-element along the person's construct dimensions. This idea would help account for the observation that the con- struct *like me in character* can be one of the most unstable in measurement terms, in contrast to the ideal self-construct (*like I'd like to be in character*), which tends to be extremely stable over time. Since the self can be viewed as an element which can be placed along many construct dimensions, it is not so surprising that in some contexts it sits on one set of dimensions and in other contexts on another set. In the context of his work a man may see himself as forceful, a good leader and full of initiative, while in the home he might see himself as kindly, a comforter and someone who falls in with the family wishes. A person can see himself as a stutterer in the context of talking to people but in more general contexts he sees himself as quite different from the group of 'stutterers'.

There is some suggestion (Smail, 1970) that a person's choice of symptom could be related to how he sees himself in relation to others. It was found that people who give more 'objective' constructs during the elicitation procedure of a repertory grid (such as *male* versus *female*; *old* versus *young*) are more likely to have somatic symptoms, whereas those producing more 'psychological' constructs (such as *easy-going* versus *strict, brash* versus *quiet*) favour psychological symptoms. Additionally to this, previous work (Caine and Smail, 1969a and 1969b) indicates that preferences for certain types of treatment among psychiatrists and nurses depend more on their personal construing of life than on any medical arguments.

Change in the individual

Bannister and Bott (1971) are conducting a series of treatment studies in which both the evaluation and understanding of the complaint and statements of expected change are examined in grid terms. Grid results dictate the lines along which treatment proceeds. The following is a characteristic case.

Following an industrial accident which left him a semi-cripple with an artificial leg, the patient became severely depressed, subject to outbursts of intense anger, suffered from headaches, was tense, uninterested in his leisure and unable to contemplate further work. Psychotherapy was begun and it was focused on the problem of helping the patient to adjust to the idea of himself as 'a man with a wooden leg' and to recover from what the patient and the therapist thought of as the consequences of the accident. For a longish period psychotherapy was markedly unsuccessful and eventually the patient was given a grid in an attempt to understand better the way in which he saw himself and other people.

For this grid, the patient made judgements about ten people who were important in his life – his wife, a close friend, a person towards whom he had always been antagonistic and so on. The names of the people were presented to him in threes, and he was asked to state some important way in which two of them were alike and thereby different from the other. For one triad, he said: these two *have confidence in themselves,* the other *has no confidence.* This, therefore, is presumably one way in which he sees people as different from each other; it is one of the personality dimensions he considers important. In this way, fourteen constructs (two poles for each construct) were elicited and three (*like me, as I'd like to be* and *like I used to be*) were supplied by the psychologist.

On each construct-dimension, the patient rank-ordered his ten people – he put them in order, from the *most confident,* for example, down to the *least confident.* The resulting grid was analysed by working out the correlations between each rank-ordering. The patient tended to rank the same people *high* on *like I am* as he ranked *low* on *understanding.* This gave a negative correlation (-0.76) between the two constructs. This can be taken to imply that, in grid terms, he does not 'see' himself as an understanding person.

The matrix of interrelationships between all the constructs was analysed and showed clear clusters, or groups of constructs. The graphs (Figure 9) represent visually the relationship between the constructs. The nearer together the constructs in this space, the more alike they are in meaning. A similar graph of construct relationships is shown as Figure 7 (p. 143) and was derived in the same way.

The axes have been left unlabelled, but we could speculatively see Axis I as *my moral ideal* versus *opposite to my moral ideal,* judging by the way the constructs relate to it.

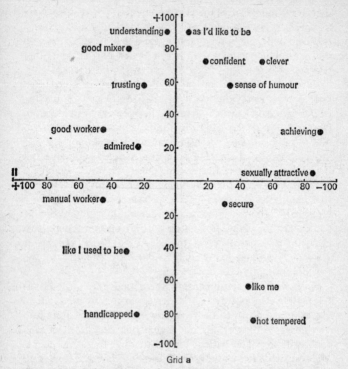

Grid **a**

Figure 9 Relationship scores along two axes for supplied and elicited constructs for one person. Grid **b** is the mirror image of **a** as it plots the contrast pole of each construct, but for the sake of clarity they are not superimposed.

Axis II is difficult to label – one pole could be labelled *my practical ideal*. Note that, in thus labelling the axes, we are following traditional practice and trying to summarize the mathematical relationships *in our own terms*. We should beware of becoming too attached to any such imposed categorization.

This patient had presented himself as a once happy and well man who now had problems all relating to an accident which had left him a cripple with an artificial leg. Yet the

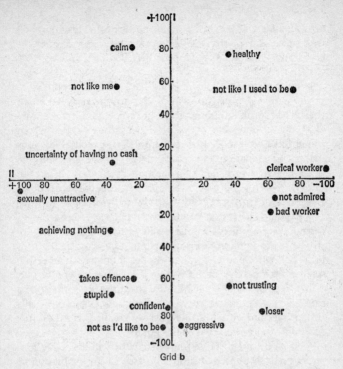

Grid b

position of *like I used to be* suggests a long-standing dis-crepancy between his picture of himself and his ideals (*as I would like to be*). Moreover, although he argued that a loss of working efficiency was the essence of his problem, his ideal was more closely related to interpersonal constructs such as *understanding*, *good mixer* and *trusting*.

Following the implications of this grid, the focus of the psychotherapy was changed. Patient and therapist began to explore the patient's relationships with other people as they had evolved throughout his lifetime. The question of work was left temporarily unanswered and the issue of 'being a man with a wooden leg' was left entirely on one side. It was assumed that however traumatic the industrial accident may have been, the problems at issue long pre-dated it and must be discussed as if they were independent of it. This approach was successful in that he elaborated his interpersonal relationships *and* adapted to the wooden leg and to new work.

It is important to bear in mind here that the argument is not that this way of formulating the problem was true and the earlier formulation was false, nor to deny that there were probably several other ways of viewing the problem which might have been more or less helpful. The essential lesson is that the formulation and reformulation of the problem, the different ways in which the question can be asked, are an integral *part* of the psychotherapeutic process itself, not an issue settled irrevocably by 'correct' diagnosis before therapy begins. The lesson presumably applies to our ways of formulating problems in our personal lives. Those who are still prone to think in terms of the 'real illness' or 'real symptom' or 'real Oedipal conflict' model should remember the science fiction story about a homicidal maniac who buys a home psychotherapy machine to cure him of killing. The salesman sells him, in error, a Martian model which succeeds in 'curing' him of a Martian psychosis called 'feem desire', after convincing him that he has got it.

Ryle and Lunghi (1969) have suggested that such a construct analysis approach should be used in the evaluation of the *outcome* of psychotherapy. Most studies of the effects of psychotherapy rest on crude, generalized measures of improvement. No one ought arbitrarily and generally to decide what is the criterion of improvement. Ryle suggests that the desired effects of any treatment should be stated beforehand *for each patient*.

Change in a couple

Another approach to the study of outcome focuses on the degree of closeness of the complainer and helper's use of certain constructs. Cartwright and Lerner (1963) found that patients having client-centred Rogerian therapy were more likely to improve if the therapist increased his 'understanding' of them during treatment. Understanding or empathy was measured by the similarity between the patient's construing of himself (using ten elicited constructs) and the therapist's use of these constructs in role playing the patient. Additionally, a client was more likely to improve if he saw a 'need to change', this being the difference between how he saw himself at the start of treatment and how he hoped to be at the end. Landfield (1971) found, using grids, that therapists who used their patients' construing language were less likely to have them opt out of treatment.

While the investigation of the similarities in construing of client and clinician could be said to be dyadic in nature, the primary focus is the client. Drewery and Rae (1969) used a dyadic approach they called the Interpersonal Perception Technique to help understand the relationships between alcoholics and their spouses. Both husband and wife filled in a personality questionnaire (the Edwards Personal Preference Schedule) from the point of view of 'Myself as I am', 'My spouse as I see him/her' and 'Myself as I think my spouse sees me'. A control group also completed these questionnaires and the most important difference between the control couples and the alcoholic partners lay in the husband's self-description compared with his wife's view of him. The control husbands and wives shared a well-defined idea of masculinity, which was free from internal inconsistencies, while the alcoholic pairs did not. The alcoholics see themselves as more feminine and their wives as more masculine. The 'alcoholic' wife sees her huband as a man with a great need to help others, to be independent and aggressive, at the same time feeling dependent on the help and friendship of others, so having considerable conflict. The husband himself sees no such conflict, but sees himself as generally more feminine. Drewery and Rae interpret this as an attempt to 'minimise his neurotic difficulties by denying his needs for autonomy and control'. This interpretation is strengthened by the evidence that it is this rejected aspect of his personality which he ascribes to his wife, attributing to her the dominance and aggression which he does not accept in himself.

Bannister and Bott (1971) have taken this type of study of

interpersonal perception between husband and wife a step further in using it as the basis of marriage counselling. They elicited constructs from both partners and asked them to use these independently in a form of rank order grid. Both sets of constructs were then combined into one grid and the couple completed the grid *together*. This procedure of obtaining two independent grids and a joint grid was repeated several times throughout counselling; the separate grids were correlated with the 'duo' grid to show who was the dominant partner. Dominance proved to be related to the absence or presence of any sexual contact (the primary problem). When the husband was dominant, sexual contact was taboo and when the wife was dominant, as at the second testing occasion, increasing sexual contact was noted (see Table 2).

Table 2

Correlations between Single Grids of a Husband and Wife with their 'Duo' Grid and the Relation of These to their Level of Sexual Activity

Occasions	Husband	Wife	
1	0·59	0·09	Sexual activity nil
2	0·19	0·64	Sexually active
3	0·33	0·48	Sexual activity decreasing
4	0·83	0·56	Sexual activity almost nil

Source: Bannister and Bott (1971)

Ryle and Lunghi (1970) commented that constructs elicited from people attending for psychiatric help most often relate to interpersonal behaviour, but are then applied to elements in general. They give the example 'in rating John on the construct "is understanding", the rater must make an overall judgement which might take no account of John's relative lack of understanding of Jill, or of his exceptional understanding of Elizabeth'. They therefore developed a 'dyad grid' in which the elements are relationships and not individuals (e.g. John in relation to Jill, John in relation to

Elizabeth and so forth). This is a very interesting development and could well prove extremely useful in the study of marriage problems which so often involve conflicts in interpersonal relationships of the sort just described.

Change in the group

Personal problems are often seen as a breakdown in social relationships and so it seems logical that these problems should be sorted out in a social setting. Group psychotherapy has evolved largely to provide such a social setting.

A great deal that has been written on the subject has been of the pontificating rather than the inquiring kind. Where inquiries have been made, often little more is gained than information about how much various members talk, or what the verb to adjective ratio is (e.g. Sechrest and Barger, 1961). There have been a few attempts to go deeper than this, such as those applying the notions of empathy, warmth and genuineness to outcome (Truax, 1961; Truax *et al.*, 1965).

Little work has been carried out on the group process based on Kelly's theory although he described six stages through which the group could be guided to enable each member of the group ultimately to stand on his own feet without group support. These stages include acceptance or 'readiness to see the world through another person's eyes', group role-playing within the confines of the group, to enactment of situations outside the group and finally experimenting with roles outside the group.

Two studies have recently been reported in which the theory and grid method were used to study group processes (Fransella and Joyston-Bechal, 1971; Fransella, 1970b; and Watson, 1970). These investigators all used the members of the group as elements. That is, each member of the group rated or ranked himself along with others in the group in terms of certain constructs. In each case the verbal labels were supplied by the investigators. Although this supplying of adjectives is not desirable if the aim is to get to know the specific constructs of individual group members, in practice it would be extremely difficult to make content comparisons across group members without standardizing the verbal labels. (It should be remembered that the construct–discriminations are not supplied, only words which the subject interprets in terms of *his* constructs.)

Interesting things happen when change in process as well as content is looked at. It appears that changes along the tight–loose dimension can occur during group psychotherapy among the majority of members. Not only this, but the changes happen *at the same time*. Further, they are not limited to those actively participating in the discussions, but include the person who sits silently present in order to make an 'objective' assessment of what has occurred (Fransella and Joyston-Bechal, 1971). Figure 5 shows the degree to which this has occurred in one group over one year. That some such fluctuation occurs is not a new idea (e.g. Rogers, 1958; Walker *et al.*, 1960; Argyris, 1969), but construct theory enables hypotheses concerning its occurrence to be made and possible causal relationships to be investigated. Argyris (1969) has commented that successful T-groups move from 'tight' to 'loose' construing during the course of their meetings. Perhaps by looking at this through construct theory goggles we can hope to find out why they are successful.

Fransella and Joyston-Bechal (1971) describe two other measures that are of value when studying group process. One is a measure of two sorts of change that can occur on grids when group members are used by each other as elements. A person can change from seeing status as being a desirable quality because it carries with it *respect from others, intelligence, power, wisdom* and *integrity*, to seeing it as something that usually goes with *power* and *money* but only sometimes with *intelligence* and *respect*; some people with high status are definitely not worthy of respect and are downright rude and stupid. Alternatively, the person can hang on to his idea of what constitutes status but change the people in the group from one end of the dimension to the other. Apparent change in group attitudes seems often to be of this latter sort. In the study in question, the group members *and the psychiatrist* changed their views of each other quite dramatically during the course of the year, but the relationship *between the constructs* changed little. These are thus measures of the degree to which the group and its individual members view the world differently at the end of the meetings, or merely see each other differently.

The other was a measure of the extent to which each person was able to perceive how the other members saw him. For most of the group, people who saw themselves as being *like the therapist* were so seen by the group. On the other hand, they were most inaccurate in perceiving, or admitting to perceiving, that they were *disliked*. The only two people showing a significantly rated therapeutic improvement were the two who were *most* accurate in seeing how others saw them in terms of the constructs used in the grid. They were also the people who had no significant fluctuation over time in their tightness of construing.

There was a tendency for the psychiatrist to see 'tight' construing as contra-indicating improvement. Most theoretical positions support this view, but it was surprising that he considered *accuracy* of perceiving how others saw them as contra-indicating improvement. The picture gets even more cloudy when we consider that the only two people who were judged *by independent judges* to have improved were two who did not vary on the 'tight-loose' dimension and who were most *accurate* in perceiving how others saw them.

A closer look at how the psychiatrist construed improvement would have helped, but could not be managed because of the use of supplied construct labels. However, McPherson and Walton (1970) directly studied psychiatrists' construing of people in group psychotherapy. They gave grids with elicited constructs to clinicians who had observed at least twenty-five meetings of a single psychotherapy group. These were combined into a single grid which was analysed into its principal components (Slater, 1964). The first component was *dominance–submissiveness*; the second *emotionally sensitive to others – emotionally insensitive to others* and the third *hinders attainment of group goals – aids attainment of group goals.* The second component contains constructs such as *ability to feel with others – involved only with self; sensitive to others' feelings – insensitive to others' feelings.* It may be that the psychiatrist in the Fransella and Joyston-Bechal study was using this second dimension and saw sensitivity of *feeling* as indicating improvement while regarding accuracy of *perception* as contra-indicating improvement. Results such as these support the contention that construct theory and grid technique may help shed light, not only on individual problems, but also on processes underlying group interaction.

Purposes in psychotherapy

Kelly saw the purpose of psychotherapy as liberation – it should enable the client to escape from the imprisoning contradictions of his own view of life. He summarized kinds of personal re-invention in psychotherapy as follows.

The team of client and therapist can go about their task in a variety of ways. Essentially these are the same ways that, on one occasion or another, man has always employed for dealing with perplexities. (1) The two of them can decide that the client should reverse his position with respect to one of the more obvious reference axes. Call this slot rattling, if you please. It has its place. (2) Or they can select another construct from the client's ready repertory and apply it to matters at hand. This, also, is a rather straightforward approach. Usually the client has already tried it. (3) They can make more explicit those preverbal constructs by which all of us order our lives in considerable degree. Some think of this as dredging the unconscious. The figure is one that a few have found useful; but I would prefer not to use it. (4) They can elaborate the construct system to test it for internal consistency. (5) They can test constructs for their predictive validity. (6) They can increase the range of convenience of certain constructs, that is, apply them more generally. They can also decrease the range of convenience and thus reduce a construct to a kind of obsolescence. (7) They can alter the meaning of certain constructs; rotate the reference axes. (8) They can erect new reference axes. This is the most ambitious undertaking of all (Kelly, 1969, p. 231).

In evaluating how broad are the implications of these prescriptions for change, be it noted that Salmon and Bannister
(1969) found them useful as a formula for inspiring the
teacher in the classroom. The techniques used for achieving
these kinds of change can range through behavioural ex-
ercises, free association, role playing and many not yet invented. The unchanging theme of the approach is the
partnership it prescribes for 'therapist' and 'client' and the
contructs of process it provides. These are abstract enough
to subsume the diverse multitude of personal concerns which
people in therapy will present and reasonably hope to have
understood.

7 The Person as Thinker

Speaking generally, the causation of insanity everywhere,
special organic diseases apart, is an affair of the three w's – worry,
want and wickedness. Its cure is a matter of three m's – method,
meat and morality.

Report of the Lancet Commission on Lunatic Asylums, 1875

One of the prime effects of carrying out research within a
specific theoretical framework is that the theory decides the
questions that are to be asked. A well-elaborated theory
should not only provide the research with a language and a
methodology but should indicate what issues are fundamental. The tie-up between a theory and the questions
that one asks is obvious enough. If in England someone asks
you, within ten minutes of becoming acquainted, what
school you went to, you can make a reasonable inference
back from that question to the kind of social theory that the
questioner is walking around with; a theory which argues
that type of school indicates social class membership; social
class membership indicates a multitude of probable attitudes;
and so forth. Not only does theory generate issues for experimental investigation, but it asks its questions in a sequential way so that each answer elaborates a continuous and
developing line of argument.

This chapter is devoted first to a description of a long-term
research into what is known as schizophrenic thought disorder, for the purpose of illustrating the systematizing and
language-providing qualities of personal construct theory
for the research worker. Following this, the capacity
of the theory to generate speculations in other areas of so-
called abnormal psychology will be exemplified. Within the

unified framework of personal construct theory, normal and abnormal are not two psychologies, they are merely different possibilities described in the same terms.

Schizophrenic thought disorder

A thought-disordered schizophrenic once sent the following question to the BBC Brains Trust.

A Darwinian biologist in the Greco-Roman war escapes by studying Afro-Asian sociology in a Grecian way and social sciences in a Roman way; Wolfenden is the Chairman of the National Social Council. What is the future of the branch of this tree? I am an Air Force blue mouse.

While admiring the poetic qualities of the question (poetry is another form of loose construing, as is dreaming by day or by night), it can be argued to be an unfair question.

Clinical descriptions of schizophrenic thought disorder stress that it is marked by vagueness, irrelevance, poverty of content and so forth and that the sum of such qualities, in the experience of the listener, is incomprehensibility. In construct theory terms, the primary question concerning 'incomprehensibility' is whether it stems from the use of a private language by the speaker or whether there is no language at all but just 'noise'. We all accept that well constructed and systematic construct subsystems may be incomprehensible to us. An atomic physicist discoursing on the deeper mysteries of his subject may be, to most of us, incomprehensible, but we do not therefore judge him to be a thought-disordered schizophrenic. We accept that he is probably saying something very meaningful and that it is we who lack the necessary construct *subsystem* to enable us to understand him. The shortcoming is ours not his.

Construct theory not only makes *meaning* versus *noise* a prime issue in the context of thought disorder, but it offers a mode of attack on the problem. Repertory grids, however much they may vary in content and form, are designed to show the relationships *between* a subject's responses in mathematical terms. They provide signs of a system of categories and, quite without reference to any particular content, they can reveal organization, or lack of it, in the person's construing. A series of experiments (Bannister, 1960 and 1962a; Bannister and Fransella, 1966; Foulds *et al*, 1967) indicated that thought-disordered schizophrenics suffer from a gross loosening of construing. This was shown by the fact that the mathematical relationships between the constructs were low and the pattern of relationships between the constructs was unstable over time – thought-disordered schizophrenics lack conceptual structure and consistency. In contrast, grids which were repeatedly given to groups of non thought-disordered schizophrenics, normals, neurotics, people with brain damage, depressives and so forth, showed significantly higher relationships between constructs and the pattern of these relationships remained consistent across new grids with varying elements.

A key aspect of grids in this context is that they provide us with a method of assessing degree of structure and organization in construing without dragging us into the different issue of whether the person's construing is 'right' or 'wrong'. We do not have to make our criterion of disorder a normative one, but can separate the question of 'Does the person have an organized way of viewing his life?' from the quite different question of 'Is the subject's organized way of viewing life like other people's, and is it one that I, the experimenter, deem sensible?'

The first question of *noise* versus *meaning* arises out of the construct theory notion of a construct *system*. A second question stems from the construct theory idea of construct *subsystems*. In construct theory it is accepted that any construct has a limited range of convenience and that whole clusters of constructs are designed to deal with particular areas, e.g. chemistry, theology, music, politics and so forth. A subsystem can be defined as a cluster of constructs within which high interrelationships exist while there are relatively few linkages between this and other subsystems of constructs. Theoretically at least, there is no reason to assume that all subsystems will have the same structural qualities. In everyday experience most of us have encountered, say, the kind of man who has a magnificently elaborated and com-

plex subsystem for construing motor cars, but who is bar-
barically simple in his construing of people.

Thus, construct theory research into schizophrenic
thought disorder must, sooner or later, face the question of
whether schizophrenics are disordered across their whole
construct system or whether the disorder is focal. Are
thought-disordered schizophrenics equally perplexed by
every aspect of the world in which they live or do some kinds
of things perplex them much more than others? This question was posed in a crude form by setting up an experiment
to explore differences in the construing of 'people' and of
'objects' by thought-disordered schizophrenics and people
with no obvious psychiatric disorder (Bannister and Salmon,
1966). Comparable grids were devised so that in the first grid
the elements were photographs of people to be construed on
psychological constructs such as *mean, kind, selfish* and so
forth, while in the second grid the elements were objects (e.g.
bowler hat, drawing pin, loaf of bread) and the constructs
were those whose range of convenience is objects, such as
curved–straight, cumbersome–handy, heavy–light and so
forth. Subjects completed two equivalent grids for people
and two for objects so that both the degree of structure and
the stability of the pattern of construct interrelationships
across elements could be assessed.

The results indicated that normals construe objects in a
more structured and stable way than they construe people –
they are more confident as physicists than they are as
psychologists. It was also found that thought-disordered
schizophrenics are not as structured and stable as normals in
their construing of objects. However, the greatest difference
between the two groups lay in the discrepancy between
'object' and 'people' construing. Thought-disordered schizophrenics were only a little worse than normals in their
construing of objects but they were vastly less stable and
consistent in their construing on psychological dimensions.
This suggests that schizophrenic thought disorder may not
be diffuse, but may be particularly related to interpersonal
construing.

A subsequent experiment which points in the same direction, while using an entirely different technique, was carried out by Salmon, Bramley and Presly (1967). It appears that thought-disordered schizophrenics *are the equal of* non thought-disordered schizophrenics in guessing the meaning of 'object' words from their context, but less capable in guessing the meaning of 'psychological' words. Obviously, this kind of experiment needs a great deal of replication and elaboration before we can deal with such complicating issues as 'difficulty level'. If it is interpersonal construing that has been specifically damaged in thought-disorder, then any theory about its origins would have to take account of this. Theories of the 'schizococcus' would perhaps have to postulate a bug that bites 'person thinking' rather than 'object thinking' brain cells.

A further question arises out of the stress that construct theory places on process and change. Construct theory is almost the exact inverse of trait theories of personality in that it specifically argues that man is a form of motion and not a static object that is occasionally kicked into movement. Thus, very rapidly, any construct theory research on schizophrenic thought-disorder (and this would apply equally to construct theory research in other areas) is forced to face the question of how do people *become* thought-disordered. It is not enough to give an account of the condition as it stands and simply assert that it is all due to, say, a defective 'filter mechanism'. A whole series of ideas need to be put forward to account for the transition from ordered to disordered thinking.

Additionally, since construct theory is not a theory of schizophrenic thought-disorder but a theory of normal psychological functioning, these hypotheses will inevitably relate to thinking processes in normal people. There are barely a dozen references in the whole of Kelly's 1200-page work to schizophrenia as such, although in practice it can be shown that schizophrenic thought-disorder falls well within the *range* of *convenience* of the theory.

The initial crude hypothesis set up for test was that schizophrenic thought-disorder is the ultimate outcome of the experience of *serial invalidation*. It was argued that there are a number of ways we could handle the experience of being wrong in our predictions – for example slot change, in which we re-view the element as the contrast of our expectation (John is *hating* not *loving*); shift change, in which we attempt to re-construe in terms of some other construct (John is *discourteous* rather than *courteous* and neither *hating* nor *loving*); structural change, in which links between the constructs are altered (true, John is *inconsiderate* but *consideration* is not an essential part of *loving*). However if, in spite of varying our strategies, we continue to be proved wrong in our expectations, it may be necessary for us to loosen the links between our constructs so that our system no longer gives rise to such uni-directional, brittle and testable anticipations. This grossly loosened construing places us in a position where we cannot, in our own terms, be wrong. It is equally true that with such a vague conceptualization of our life, we cannot, in any very specific sense, be right. It should be noted that loosening and tightening are not of themselves pathological reactions, but are normal reactions to varying validational fortunes. What is being argued is that the thought-disordered schizophrenic has been driven to loosen *beyond the point* at which there are enough workable lines of implication between his constructs for him to re-tighten his system. He has sawn off the psychological branch on which he was sitting.

As a laboratory test of this hypothesis, experiments were conducted in which people were serially invalidated (Bannister, 1963 and 1965). People were presented with a series of photographs and told that their judgement of personality from faces was under test. In all the experimental trials each person was faced by a group of photographs and he was asked to rank order them on a set of supplied constructs (i.e. he put his ten photographs in order from the most to least *generous,* most to least *intelligent* and so forth). Correlations (Spearman rhos) were calculated between his series of rank orders to indicate the degree of structure implied by the ranking. In succeeding trials new sets of photographs were presented to be rank ordered on the same set of constructs and for each trial the *level of intercorrelation* between the rankings was noted. If the subject was in a serially validated group, he was told on each occasion that his judgements were very accurate and fake life histories of the photographed people were often supplied to substantiate this. If the subject was in a serially invalidated group, he was told that he was doing badly and that his judgements were largely *inaccurate*. In some of the experiments base lines were obtained by having a no information group.

The experiments showed that successively telling a person he was *right* caused him to tighten his construing; the intercorrelations between his constructs rose steadily from trial to trial. Ultimately, these 'right' people were putting their photographs in virtually the same order on all 'good' adjectives and in reverse order on all 'bad' adjectives – thus they were using their constructs as one single superordinate construct. The people did not seem to be aware of this fact, perhaps because they were convinced that what mattered was the actual judgement made on each photograph on each construct and did not seem aware that the focus of interest was the *interrelationship* between the constructs themselves. Yet tightening of this type can be construed as a meaningful process. If we have an implicit theory that is working wellnigh perfectly in some area of construing, then the only change that may seem worth making is to simplify the theory and see if it works just as well – in this respect people taking part in the experiment seemed to have been following the law of parsimony.

On the other hand, when the people in the experiment were successively told they were wrong, they did not seem in the early stages to loosen the interrelationships between their constructs. But they did respond markedly with another strategy – they changed the *pattern* of interrelationships. Thus, one person completed his ninth grid to show that *kind* and *sincere* were highly positively correlated (0·70) while on the tenth grid these two constructs were shown as highly negatively correlated (−0·90). This wild swinging of the pattern of relationships between constructs seems to be an initial and marked reaction to invalidation. However, in the final experiment it was shown that if one cluster of constructs at a time rather than the whole sub-system at once was invalidated, then loosening took place. Although this is an artificial and laboratory model of the process of serial invalidation, it produced movement towards the gross loosening found in thought-disordered schizophrenics. It suggests that thought-disordered people have been wrong too often. They are like scientists whose theories have been so often disproved that they have gone out of the theory making business.

Equally, the outcome of construct theory's emphasis on process is the question of how thought-disordered schizophrenics again achieve ordered thinking.

In terms of the general construct theory argument the obvious initial hypothesis is that reduction of thought-disorder ought to take place as a result of serial *validation*. In construct theory terms, validation or invalidation happen in terms of the person's *own construct system*. This is one way in which construct theory is radically different from the notion of reinforcement theory. The traditional reinforcing cigarettes of the operant conditioning programmes would only constitute validation if the patient receiving them saw the gift of cigarettes as *personally* meaningful and appropriate in that situation.

Most of what happens to thought-disordered schizophrenics interpersonally means nothing to them – in a fundamental sense it does not *happen* at all for them, because they have no way of making sense of it. It cannot be evidence on which they can more strongly structure their system. This meant that the programme for experimental modification of thought-disorder had to begin by a very extensive search of the individual schizophrenic's construct system for dealing with people. The aim was to find some residual structure, some group of still semi-clustered constructs, some echo of a half-remembered theme which would serve as a starting point for an elaboration of the system. It was through this kind of residual focus that the thought-disordered schizophrenic was encouraged to 'see' the people around him and start having expectations about them. He was then encouraged to experiment with his environment in order to test out the implications of his construing. Initially efforts were made to shield him from the experience of invalidation until the embryo system had begun to extend and define so that it could deal with invalidation. The final outcome of this research is not yet known, but its implications for other kinds of research can be seen. The 'serial invalidation' hypothesis concerning the origin of schizophrenic thought-disorder can be related to a number of psychological theories. In particular, it can be related to theories of the schizophrenic family – theories which propose destructive family interaction as the cause of 'schizophrenia'. These include the 'double bind' hypothesis of Bateson *et al.* (1956); the arguments concerning the disintegrating effects of 'mystification' by forms of family process as put forward by Laing and Esterson (1964) and the arguments which relate schizophrenia to parental 'inculcation of confused and distorted meanings' (Lidz, 1964). All these people see the processes resulting in 'schizophrenia', as having originated in the family. It can be argued that these are a series of descriptions of interpersonal events which can be included in the more general concept of serial invalidation. For example, the 'double bind' situation is one in which the 'victim' subjected to the 'bind' receives two separate but conflicting messages of a kind that cannot be ignored and where the contradiction is not self-evident, e.g. at its simplest level the statement 'of course I'm not offended' delivered in a tone which says the reverse. In construct theory terms we could argue that the person is faced with behaviour which invites two constructions either of which will then be proved wrong and neither of which provides any basis for effective anticipation of ensuing events.

There seem to be two difficulties with schizophrenogenic family theories as they are usually proposed. Firstly, we may accept that the family is vital in that grossly inconsistent behaviour by parents may lead to the development of an inadequate construing system in the child. However, we do not need to base our explanation of psychological disturbance on the family group. There are many other social situations which may prove seriously invalidating for particular individuals. The situation of admission to psychiatric hospital itself may provide yet a further series of invalidations. The experience of having your personal philosophy called an illness, of having strange characters insist that you make designs out of coloured blocks, of having an intake of drugs which may produce weird sensory distortions, of being surrounded by other 'mad' people and a staff who humour you by behaving a little madly themselves, and so forth, can be viewed as an impressive experiment in serial invalidation, likely to disrupt all but the most well articulated construct systems.

Secondly, schizophrenogenic family theories tend to focus on the plight of the potential schizophrenic and the strategies which he is forced to adopt when victimized by his family. The question of why the others are behaving as they do is inadequately considered. Why do double-binders double bind, mystifiers mystify and teachers of distorted meanings teach such meanings? From a construct theory viewpoint, the interpersonal situation should be considered in role relationship terms so that we can explain the behaviour of both members of a pair or all members of a relevant larger group. The problem might be looked at in terms of those role relationships (victor and vanquished, master and slave, straight-man and stooge, doctor and patient, teacher and student and so forth) which *may* demand the confusion of the one partner, in order to allow the other to define his clarity by contrast.

A further question about the causes of 'schizophrenia' concerns the construing strategies which may precede thought-disorder. In the serial invalidation experiments the most notable initial reaction was a marked alteration in the *pattern* of construct relationships; a repeated revision of the person's idea of what qualities went with what. The effect of such revisions on a large scale is inevitably to produce a pattern of construct relationships which is markedly idiosyncratic and measurably discrepant from the construct linkages we would normally expect. The person might thus acquire unusual meanings for his concepts and an 'odd' personality theory. It could be argued that paranoid thinking may be of this type. The paranoid person with his ideas of persecution, grandiosity and so forth may have an organized way of viewing the world, but it is a peculiar view; he has a dictionary but it is a private dictionary. If such were the case, then very serious communication difficulties would occur. The owner of the idiosyncratic system might find it very difficult to form relationships with other people or to use them as guides to his own identity – hence the essential isolation of the paranoid person.

This leaves open the question of why, if paranoia is a bus stop on the way to schizophrenic thought-disorder, some get off the bus there, while others carry on to thought-disorder. The answer may lie in the original state of development of the construct system at 'point of impact'. Thought-disorder may be the fate of the person whose construct system had never developed beyond a relatively embryonic level and paranoia may be the result of pressures on a construct system which was largely workable until particular interpersonal difficulties were met. This idea is explored in Bannister, Fransella and Agnew (1971) and the whole line of research may help to break down the global and unworkable ragbag concept of 'schizophrenia'.

Thinking in the dysphasic

If we argue that thought-disordered schizophrenics are at the 'loose' end of a 'tight–loose' continuum, then we can equally contemplate the other end of the dimension, at which a person has to force all events into a few tightly and unmodifiably related constructs. There are available to us a few hints about this 'other end'.

An attempt was made to measure the extent to which a

person who has lost the ability to speak has also lost the ability to understand what is said to him. It was argued that if such a person is able to relate up the elements in a grid test in a consistent and structured way, then he must be able to understand at least some of the things that are going on in his environment. In a study of a group of people who had various degrees of loss of speech as the result of damage to the brain (Fransella, 1970c), it was found that the scores of these people in the Grid Test of Thought Disorder (Bannister and Fransella, 1967) formed bimodal distributions. There were those who acted *as if* they were thought-disordered and there were those who gave scores at the tight end of the 'tight-loose' dimension.

Perhaps this exaggerated tightening is a reaction to the loss of speech itself. It may be a reaction to the threat and anxiety inherent in the situation. Structure must be maintained at all costs. One uncontrolled observation was rather striking. This concerned a man who was considered to be totally unable to speak and also almost totally unable to understand anything that was said to him. However, he obtained nearly the highest score possible on the Grid Test. He was certainly hanging on to *some* thought structure. To investigate this further, he was given a similar test, this time with objects (instead of photographs of people) and constructs to do with objects. This was done because most standard tests given to dysphasics have to do with the manipulation of objects. It was argued that perhaps, for some unaccountable reason, there might be selective impairment of 'object' construing as opposed to 'people' construing. This would have been interesting if it had been the case, since it would be the converse situation to that found by Bannister and Salmon (1966) with thought-disordered schizophrenics. However, it was not the case. The consistency with which the man sorted the objects as 'heaviest' or 'smoothest' and so forth was high. As a final part of the investigation he was asked to *hand over* the objects as they were named (e.g. 'ash-tray', 'piece of sandpaper', 'drinking straw'); *he was quite unable to relate the name to the object*. It seemed as if the construing system was still intact – although not very able to deal with new information – but the system had become detached from the verbal labels of elements. He could sort objects when asked to in terms of weight or smoothness and people in terms of kindness or sincerity, but could not indicate the elements by name.

Further research with other dysphasic people is being considered using 'action grids'. Perhaps structure could be demonstrated if 'weight', for instance, were asked for by sign language rather than by word. Very clearly some of these people are not as disordered in their thinking as their scores on some tests and their behaviour make them appear. They are quite able to recognize places where they should and should not walk, what ash-trays are for and to differentiate between people in behavioural terms. Perhaps their injury is such that it renders them unable to associate verbal labels with their elements.

This line of inquiry might have implications for treatment. It would focus treatment on the problem of *associating* the construct with the verbal labels of the elements within its range of convenience, rather than of building up constructs themselves.

Thinking in the obsessional

While collecting the normative data for the Grid Test of Thought Disorder, it was observed that the scores for the neurotic population were very similar to the 'normal' group except for a few who construed very 'loosely'. These consisted, in the main, of those diagnosed as suffering from obsessional neurosis (characterized by the compulsion to dwell on certain themes, often resulting in repetitive behaviour). This seemed contrary to what one might expect, but perhaps the obsessional had so constricted the construing of his environment that the only part of his system with 'tight' structure was that to do with his obsessional thoughts and acts. Subsequent uncontrolled observations suggested that this might be so. Again, it was as if the obsessional person was living in the only world that was meaningful to him – outside the area of his obsessions all was vagueness and confusion.

Kelly discusses this behaviour in relation to his fragmentation corollary.

The construct system of such a client is characteristically impermeable; he needs a separate pigeonhole for each new experience and he calculates his anticipations of events with minute pseudo-mathematical schemes. He has long been accustomed to subsume his principles. The variety of construction sub-systems which are inferentially incompatible with each other may, in the train of rapidly moving events, become so vast that he is hard put to it to find ready-made superordinate constructs which are sufficiently permeable or open-ended to maintain over-all consistency. He starts making new ones (Kelly, 1955, p. 89).

Some further information about the construing of the obsessional person has been provided by Makhlouf-Norris (1968 and 1970). She elicited constructs from obsessional patients and examined ways in which these were related. Structurally, the obsessionals tended to have non-articulated systems, meaning that there was one dominant cluster of constructs or else there were several primary clusters with no linking constructs between the clusters. Examples of a 'monolithic' structure of an obsessional patient and an 'articulated' system of a normal person are shown in Figures 10 and 11. A cluster is defined as a group of constructs which all significantly correlate with one another; a linkage construct is one which is significantly correlated with constructs in *two* or *more* clusters.

The number of inferences which the obsessional could make across clusters with his 'monolithic' system was limited – he had a 'compartmentalized' mind. No difference was found in the overall degree to which the constructs were related but the obsessionals rated themselves significantly more extremely on constellatory constructs (those that fix the realm membership of their elements) and their self constructs 'anchored' the system – they tended to interpret events along dimensions particularly used to construe the self.

Makhlouf-Norris's study has important implications for

those working with the complexity-simplicity notion. An obsessional who had, say, three separate clusters of constructs would appear to be complex in orthodox terms, but as Makhlouf-Norris pointed out, he would be functioning very 'simply' in terms of the number of inferences that he could make across constructs. Cognitive complexity is not a trait, and therefore it is quite in order to postulate that a person

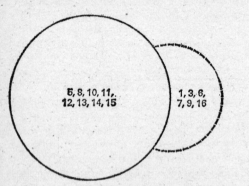

Figure 10 The monolithic construing structure of an obsessional patient. Eight numbered constructs form the primary cluster and six others the secondary cluster. The remaining two are isolates
(From Makhlouf-Norris, Jones and Norris, 1970)

can have part of his system consisting of constellatory, tight constructs and other parts of the system holding together extremely loosely.

What was not teased out in the Makhlouf-Norris study was the importance of being neurotic; the control group consisted of non-psychiatric people. There is evidence that people with clearly defined psychological abnormalities or who are neurotic in some general sense do tend to have higher Intensity scores on the Grid Test of Thought Disorder (Bannister, Fransella and Agnew, 1971) and some at least have simple or uni-dimensional subsystems to do with their particular complaints.

Thinking about the complaint

In two single case studies of obesity (Fransella, 1970d, and Fransella and Crisp, 1971) it was suggested that whether a system was unidimensional or not might be of prognostic importance. The person who has only one main channel along which to construe events will be less likely to change

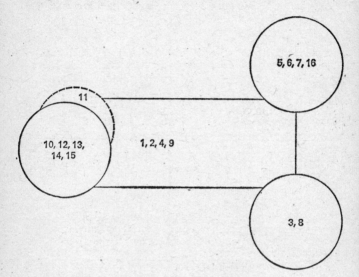

Figure 11 The articulated construing structure of a non-psychiatric person. There are three primary clusters, one with a secondary construct and a linkage cluster joining all together
(From Makhlouf-Norris, Jones and Norris, 1970)

than someone who has several avenues open to him. As well as showing 'unidimensionality', Figure 12 shows how the person's view of himself as he is at the present time can move up and down this single dimension, or 'slot-rattle' to use Kelly's more colourful language. A later grid showed a picture almost identical to that of the first grid.

Figure 13 shows how the positioning of the self along the

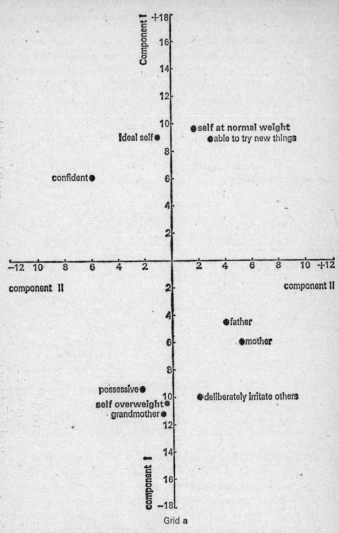

Figure 12 Principal component analysis loadings of constructs on a repertory grid for an obese woman a at the start of treatment and b five months later
(From Fransella, 1970d)

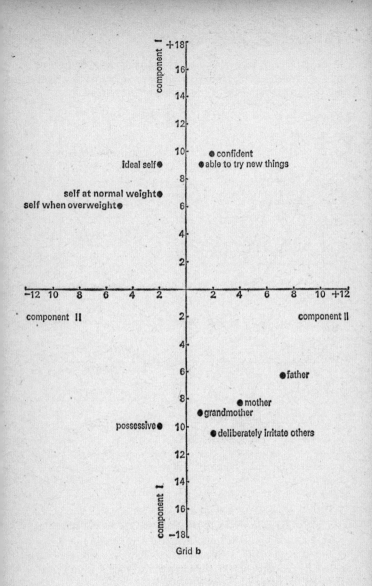

Grid b

main dimension was related to weight change. A feature of this relationship is that the change from weight loss to weight gain came *after* change in construing of the self.

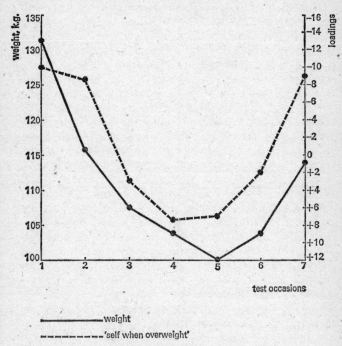

Figure 13 Relationship between weight change and the importance in construing of the 'self when overweight' construct in an obese woman
(From Fransella and Crisp, 1971)

It remains to be seen just how characteristic this simplicity of construing is in neurotic people. Perhaps people who are judged neurotic concentrate their thinking or simplify their thinking in this way. If life becomes difficult or one way of behaving becomes particularly important, then this may lead to a simplification of the whole system.

A construct theory approach to the treatment of stuttering

was based on the idea that the stutterer knows too much about his problem; what he needs to learn about is what life would be like without it. If this idea were speculatively extended to cover the obese person, the obsessional, in fact all neurotics, then many present systems of psychotherapy could be regarded as harmful. They tend to concentrate on the symptom itself, thus possibly making the person's construing even more unidimensional, restricting further its range of convenience.

One thing we know about the stutterer's construct system is that there is a significant shift in the meaningfulness of being a 'stutterer' to that of being a 'non-stutterer' in those who come to speak more fluently (see Figure 6). In addition to this, analyses of these *subsystems* reveal differences between those who improve and those who do not improve or who leave treatment prematurely. A measure of 'saturation' was devised. Degree of saturation was defined as the percentage of implications actually found in a grid to the number possible in a grid of that size.

Non-improvers had significantly higher saturation of stutterer constructs and to a lesser extent non-stutterer constructs than did improvers. This implies that those who improved to a considerable extent had less highly organized construct systems to do with themselves as speakers – there was more room for conceptual manoeuvre. Figure 14 shows comparisons in degree of 'saturation' in construing of their stuttering and non-stuttering selves for those who did not improve. 'Non-improvers' in Figure 14a started out with a more tightly structured 'stutterer' subsystem – both superordinately and subordinately – and they tightened this still further after several weeks of treatment. The 'saturation' of their superordinate 'non-stutterer' construing (Figure 14b) did not differ at the outset from the 'non-improvers', but a tremendous tightening occurred during the following weeks, contrary to that for 'improvers'.

Figure 15 shows two individuals, one who improved and one who did not improve and then stopped treatment. Both initially tended to tighten their construing, but the

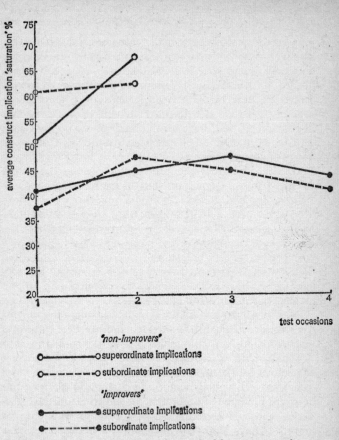

Figure 14a Per cent implications 'saturation' for stutterers who improved or did not improve (or withdrew from treatment) on Impgrids for **a** 'stutterer' and **b** 'non-stutterer' construing (From Fransella, 1971)

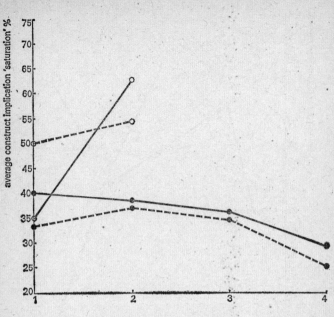

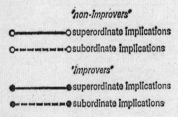

'non-improvers'

○———————○ superordinate implications

○— — — —○ subordinate implications

'improvers'

●———————● superordinate implications

●— — — —● subordinate implications

Figure 14b

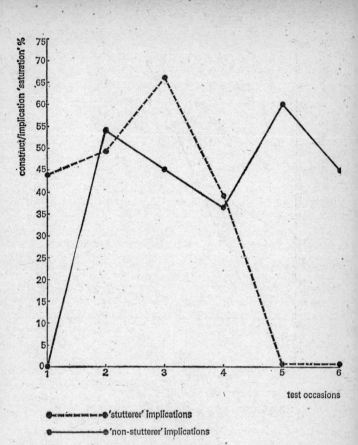

Figure 15a Per cent implication 'saturation' for a stutterer who
a improved and one who **b** did not improve on Impgrids for
'stutterer' and 'non-stutterer' construing
(From Fransella, 1971)

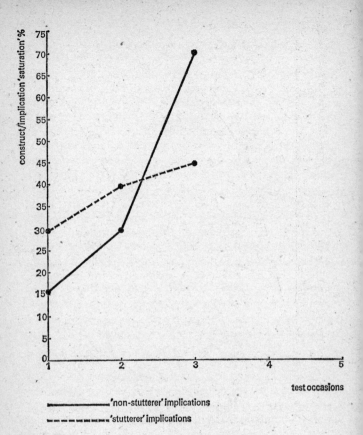

Figure 15b

'non-improver' (Figure 15b) continued to do so while the 'improver' (Figure 15a) showed considerable fluctuation, particularly in the construing of himself as a fluent speaker.

It seems possible that premature tightening of a subsystem militates against further change. This finding must be interpreted in relation to another – that 'improvers' tended to have more 'non-stutterer' implications and constructs at the start of treatment. Thus, people with a greater *absolute* number of constructs and implications but with relatively fewer implications per construct are less likely prematurely to tighten their subsystem before fluency has been firmly established. Perhaps with a small, tightly knit system, the person can only deal with a limited amount of new evidence at a time and calls a halt before being overwhelmed – it may be he is less well equipped to deal with some disquieting answers that his experiments with fluency have given him. Whether such a sequence of events occurs in others with long-standing problems remains to be seen. Formal experiments of the psychologist as well as informal experiments by people in general often provide more questions than answers.

A thought about thinking

Although, as a gesture to conventional categories, this chapter was headed 'the person as thinker', it is contended that fragmenting man into boxes of 'thinking', 'feeling', 'doing' (more pompously 'cognition', 'emotion', 'behaviour') is a bad practice. It leaves us in the predicament of Makhlouf-Norris's obsessionals, short on inferences about persons as whole persons. Feeling can be looked on as the name given to a kind of (legitimate) thinking, and doing as the experimental criterion of thinking – and this makes 'construing' a much larger construct than 'thinking'.

8 A Personal Psychology

When the behaviourist observes the doings of animals, and decides whether these show knowledge or error, he is not thinking of himself as an animal, but as an at least hypothetically inerrant recorder of what actually happens. He 'knows' that animals are deceived by mirrors, and believes himself to 'know' that *he* is not being similarly deceived. By omitting the fact that *he* – an organism like any other – is observing, he gives a false air of objectivity to the results of his observation. As soon as we remember the possible fallibility of the observer, we have introduced the serpent into the behaviourist's paradise. The serpent whispers doubts, and has no difficulty in quoting scientific scripture for the purpose.

Scientific scripture, in its most canonical form, is embodied in physics (including physiology). Physics assures us that the occurrences which we call 'perceiving objects' are at the end of a long causal chain which starts from the objects, and are not likely to resemble the objects except, at best, in certain very abstract ways. We all start from 'naïve realism', that is, the doctrine that things are what they seem. We think that grass is green, that stones are hard, and that snow is cold. But physics assures us that the greenness of grass, the hardness of stones, and the coldness of snow, are not the greenness, hardness, and coldness that we know in our own experience, but something very different. The observer, when he seems to himself to be observing a stone, is really, if physics is to be believed, observing the effects of the stone upon himself. Thus science seems to be at war with itself: when it most means to be objective, it finds itself plunged into subjectivity against its will. Naïve realism leads to physics, and physics, if true, shows that naïve realism is false. Therefore, naïve realism, if true, is false; therefore it is false. And therefore the behaviourist, when he thinks he is recording observations about the outer world, is really recording observations about what is happening to him.

BERTRAND RUSSELL, *An Inquiry into Meaning and Truth*, 1962

Many people, when first confronted by personal construct theory, see it as a denial of the generalization that 'reality is what it is and no amount of thinking will change it'. This point of view was prettily put by Bolingbroke (Shakespeare's Richard II, Act 1, Scene 3) when he had just been banished from England by the King, and his father had tried to comfort him by suggesting that he look on banishment not as an exile but as a journey of exploration, voluntarily undertaken. Bolingbroke replied as follows:

O, who can hold a fire in his hand
By thinking on the frosty Caucasus?
Or cloy the hungry edge of appetite
By bare imagination of a feast?
Or wallow naked in December snow
By thinking on fantastic summer's heat?
O, no! the apprehension of the good
Gives but the greater feeling to the worse.
Fell sorrow's tooth doth never rankle more
Than when he bites, but lanceth not the sore.

Bolingbroke, in fact, is nicely supporting one of the basic contentions of construct theory. He is stressing that constructs are bipolar and that if an element lies within the range of convenience of a construct then it must be most usefully seen at one end *or* the other – it cannot be both. The two poles of a construct have a relationship essentially of *contrast*.

But if we cannot *reverse* our view of something, this is surely not to say that we cannot *change* our view of that thing. If we go back to Gaunt's speech of comfort to his son, we will find that Bolingbroke – as is often the case with driving young men blessed with aged parents – had not listened to his father. What Gaunt had said was as follows:

Go, say I sent thee forth to purchase honour,
And not the King exil'd thee; or suppose
Devouring pestilence hangs in our air
And thou art flying to a fresher clime.
Look what thy soul holds dear, imagine it

To lie that way thou goest, not whence thou com'st.
Suppose the singing birds musicians,
The grass whereon thou tread'st the presence strew'd,
The flowers fair ladies, and thy steps no more
Than a delightful measure or a dance;
For gnarling sorrow hath less power to bite
The man that mocks at it and sets it light.

Gaunt is here opposing a pre-emptive construction of Bolingbroke's situation. He is arguing that although Bolingbroke's life abroad may be a banishment, it need not be viewed as *nothing but* a banishment. It can be viewed as a grand tour and an opportunity to explore new delights.

Very often a psychotherapist finds himself playing Gaunt to a neurotic Bolingbroke. The neurotic who is convinced that he is a slob and the rest of mankind are fine people begins by assuming that whatever new idea you suggest, or new personal venture you urge him to undertake, amounts to nothing more than the contrary assertion that he is a fine person and the rest of the world are slobs. Indeed it is by no means impossible to get him to polarize and see himself and others in this reversed light. But it is very difficult to convince the neurotic that perhaps the *slob–fine person* dichotomy is not a useful one and that there may be entirely different ways of construing, constructs at ninety degrees to his favourite, which might open up novel possibilities.

There is an old joke which tells of a yokel who was asked the way to a neighbouring town by a motorist. After describing four possible routes at great length, the yokel points out that 'If Oi were 'ee, Oi wouldn't start from 'ere'. It can be argued that the legendary yokel had made a profoundly useful point – for life if not for navigation. Thus, pondering, for example, the personal–professional problems of the uncertain psychologist, we might be tempted to doubt the wisdom of sharpening up experimental methods for manipulating the rat or the rat-sized-man or elaborating the wordy fantasies of psychoanalytic theory. We might suggest that if we were him we wouldn't start from the currently fashionable ' 'ere' in the first place.

The personal relevance of construct theory

Much has been made of the reflexive quality of personal construct theory. It has been argued that it is a theory about theories, that it treats scientists as men and men as scientists. It has been argued that in this respect it differs sharply from traditional psychological theories which do not comment on their makers as part of their subject matter. This general point was made by Bannister in the following terms.

Psychologists share the privilege of scientists in being outside the range of convenience of such theories. Granted, at a joke level psychologists may argue that a particular psycho-analyst is writing a particular paper in order to sublimate his sex instinct or we may toy with the notion that a book by some learning theorist is evidence that the said learning theorist was suffering from a build-up of reactive inhibition. But in our more solemn moments we seem to prefer the paradoxical view that psychologists are explainers, predictors and experimenters, whereas the organism, God bless him, is a very different kettle of fish.

In short, we have not yet faced up to the issue of reflexivity and the need for reflexivity in psychological thinking. If we are going to make so bold as to utter such statements as 'thinking is a matter of A and B and a little C', then such statements should equally subsume the thinking which led to them. If we are going to climb up on to platforms and make generalizations about human behaviour, then such generalizations should clearly explain the behaviour of climbing up on to platforms and making generalizations about human behaviour. The delight and instruction which many of us find in George Kelly's Personal Construct Theory derives in no small measure from the fact that it is an explicitly reflexive theory. There may be no onus on the chemist when he writes his papers on the nature of acids and alkalis to account in terms of his acid-alkali distinction for his behaviour in writing a journal paper. But psychologists are in no such fortunate position.

Turning this issue of reflexivity the other way around, I am reminded of a recurrent theme in certain types of science fiction story. The master-chemist has finally produced a bubbling green slime in his test tubes, the potential of which is great but the properties of which are mysterious. He sits alone in his laboratory, test tube in hand, brooding about what to do with the bubbling green slime. Then it slowly dawns on him that the bubbling green slime is sitting alone in the test tube brooding about what to do with him. This special nightmare of the chemist is the permanent work-a-day world of the psychologist – the bubbling green slime is always wondering what to do about you (Bannister, 1966a).

If we claim that construct theory comments intelligently on the processes of the very psychologists who use it, we are necessarily claiming that it would comment intelligently on the process of any non-professional person or psychologist who used it. Can we then exemplify how in a direct and personal sense construct theory can help resolve some of the dilemmas which seem intrinsic to the human condition?

Consider the implications of the idea of tightening and loosening as a cyclic process essential to personal development. Most of us are conscious of the need to tighten and loosen in specific situations. We may find ourselves uncomfortable in the tight and carefully arranged relationship we have with our usual snooker partner and we may back off to ponder, loosely, less specifiable issues such as what this relationship was born of, what it is now about and even why do we – him – anybody – bother with each other. And we may have noticed that when we again return to the tight questions of exactly when shall we meet to do exactly what, it is no longer all about snooker.

Yet even as many psychologists have opted permanently for a tight or a loose psychology, so many of us seem personally to have taken up residence at some fixed point in what should be a cycle. It is as if we type-cast ourselves in a general way as being *either* Cavalier or Roundhead, *either* tender-minded or tough-minded, *either* romantic or classic, *either* Koestler's Yogi or Koestler's Commissar. And for people who choose tightness or looseness as a basic posture towards life the choice has the force of a moral decision. The orderly and materialist and practical look with contempt on lives they see as half-baked and self-indulgent. The sensitive and lyrical and passionate are appalled by those they see as rule-bound and mercenary. If we mistake repetition for consistency and assumptions for reality, then we can quite easily transmute what should be different phases of living into different manners of men. And in so doing, we do not just impoverish our personal lives, we lend support to a social history which has tended to enforce these same crippling choices. Consider merely the way in which men have been moulded into being 'masculine' and women have been moulded into being 'feminine' and consider how much this has deducted from the achievements and imagination of both.

Answers beget questions

Orthodox psychologists seem to share one crucial assumption which is utterly unacceptable from a construct theory point of view. This is the assumption that man has *a nature* which we might eventually fathom and that will be that. Construct theory does not argue simply that it would be very difficult to fathom the nature of man in practice – most psychologists would admit that. It argues that it is a meaningless ideal, since the nature of individual men and of mankind is evolving and therefore can never be finally explained by any theory. The very theories which psychologists elaborate are part of this evolution of man yet some quaintly think that the journeying spirit we call man will stay still until their work is done. This is an argument worth reiterating up to and past the point of monotony. Bannister phrased it thus:

However, if we view the situation reflexively, we might be led to acknowledge that any notions that we can scrape together and articulate, our subjects, being men like us, may also scrape together and articulate. We may be, and I think we often are, faced with subjects who are formulating their lives in terms of a theory and framework as extensive and well abstracted as our own. This suggests a nice infinite regress or, more properly, infinite progress in which we elaborate a theory large enough to subsume them, they being armed only with the earlier more primitive theory, and they in turn rethink and subsume the experimenter and so goes the race. The mysterious creatures we are racing with in this context are, of course, ourselves. Such an infinite and unending elaboration is perhaps a depressing vista to those who aspire to a deterministic science in pursuit of the holy grail of final truth. It is, however, a comforting thought to those of us who fear unemployment and who like to think that every answer is as good as the question it generates (Bannister, 1966a).

Kelly (1969) phrased it more succinctly on many occasions. On one of these he spoke as follows:

Behaviour is a man's way of changing his circumstances, not proof that he has submitted to them. What on earth, then, can present day psychology be thinking about when it says that it intends only to predict and control behaviour scientifically? Does it intend to halt the human enterprise in its tracks?

He reflected on those immutable laws of behaviour:

There are, indeed, moments when I deeply suspect that man's only purpose in discovering the laws of human behaviour is to contrive some way to escape them.

But if we are to take this process view of man and see him as continually posing questions and finding answers, then we must recognize that there will be new questions inherent in the newly-found answer. The new perception and the new act which are a solution for an old problem contain in their newness the elements of our next problem.

Consider this argument as a way of looking at the curious dispute between behaviourists and psychoanalysts about 'symptom substitution'. Both behaviourists and psycho-analysts, being good, normatively-minded folk, are prepared to call certain things that people do 'symptoms' which makes it clear that, regardless of what the behaviour might mean for the person, it is going to have to be got rid of. However, behaviourists regard the 'symptom' as a maladaptive learned habit which can be unlearned and thereby utterly dispensed with. The psycho-analysts on the other hand regard the 'symptom' as a function of the person's faulty psycho-dynamics. They argue that if it is got rid of, without altering the nature of these psychodynamics, it will be replaced by another 'symptom' which will play the same part in the person's psychological economy. From a construct theory point of view, these are both very strange contentions. When a person has solved one of his problems, or to keep him in his proper station let us say we have cured him of one of his symptoms, he inevitably acquires the problems resulting from that solution. But these are not simply 'substitutions', they may well represent a substantial forward step in the personal evolution of the 'patient'. It is equally true that they *are* related to the previous 'symptom'. Consider an actual case.

The young man had a phobia for telephones and travelling. About a year of desensitization treatment enabled him to travel and use the telephone. He commented on the utter pointlessness of such an achievement since he had no one to ring up and no one to travel to. He had formed no relationships with his fellows. About two years of psychotherapeutic exploration and experimentation, and the young man was going to social gatherings, visiting his newly-found friends, was a member of this or that hobbies group. He then pointed out that no one could care less than he did for the kind of superficial social chit-chat relationships, mainly with men, which he now formed in great numbers. What he wanted was a deep, passionate, intense, sexual and exclusive relationship with a woman. And so he began ... now are we to argue that the sequential problems were no more than magical substitutes for his earlier problems, or for that matter see no connection between them?

So at a personal level, if we try to make use of construct theory, we may range it alongside a number of sources of wisdom, which teach us that we can always reconstrue but that we must accept responsibility for our constructions and for the new mysteries which they will generate.

The psychological experiment

If, as psychologists, we could forget the dreams that came with our first chemistry set, that we would ultimately be absolutely precise, Nobel prize-winning, break-through-making, socially accredited scientists of the kind that foreign governments would think it worthwhile to kidnap, then we might stop trying to mimic what we conceive to be the standard experiments of physics and begin to consider what a truly psychological experiment might be like. Even if we retained our focus on classic experiments in the natural sciences, we could pay less attention to their mathematical precision and more to their quality as acts of imagination. The vast majority of formal psychological experiments could win classification under categories such as the exquisitely obsessional or the apotheosis of the platitude, but they could hardly be called acts of imagination. Most of them were born out of the literature and, no doubt, will be buried in it.

Suppose we were to begin experimenting *with* individuals instead of *on* individuals. Suppose we were to accept that however formal and systematic the psychological experiment, it ought to be more kin to the kinds of experiments which novelists undertake with their readers, or children undertake with their parents, or lovers undertake with each other, than the kind of experiments which were undertaken by the stereotypical Victorian physicist who seems to be our current ideal. What sort of experiments might we then find ourselves engaged in? It is certain that initially they would be rather murky and quite unpublishable, but these two conditions might be no bad thing in themselves. Consider some moves in this direction.

McFall (1965) played with a form of experiment which earned itself the title of McFall's Mystical Monitor. The procedure was simple enough. You take a person (he is not a 'subject' because he is just as likely to be another psychologist or McFall himself, or someone who will decline to be part of any official sample) and you isolate him with a tape recorder and a set of suggestions. The suggestions are that he set the tape recorder running and begin to talk into it – talking about whatever comes into his head. After a period of twenty minutes or so he is to rewind the tape and play back what he has said. Then he is to begin again and talk into the tape for an hour or as long as he likes. Then he is to rewind and play through what he has said this time. He can if he wishes play it through two or three times, but the key point is that when he has finished and before he leaves the room, he *must* erase the tape completely so that no record is left. Obviously this is a variant on the time-honoured, if disreputable, custom of talking to oneself. But the gimmick of the tape adds the extra dimension of listening to oneself. And the essence of the talk is that it is talk *without an audience*. This is the reason for the first twenty-minute run which has to be listened to before the main session begins. Almost invariably people report that they were embarrassed by the first twenty minutes because they heard themselves talking *as to an audience,* they heard themselves posturing and presenting themselves, excusing themselves, concealing themselves, doing all the necessary things that we do when we have any kind of audience. But many found that listening to that first twenty minutes or so forced them into asking the inevitable question – something like 'who do I think I am kidding?' And since they obviously weren't kidding anybody, they found that the next long section of the tape represented something new – perhaps a chance to reflect on their own reflections. The absolute guarantee, made to oneself, that the tape will be erased is essential or the tape will be merely a speech to some future audience, perhaps a future self.

What were the results of McFall's experiments? From an orthodox point of view perhaps there were not really any 'results' at all. Certainly none that could be rushed into the journals at the 5 per cent level of confidence. But if we rephrase the question and say *what was learned from the experiment,* then the answer is quite a little. Most of the experimenters (and the answer to the subject-experimenter identity question may be that everyone who does this is an experimenter) claimed they had learned something from it about the central issues in their life. Even though the very nature of the experiment (not accidentally) meant the destruction of much of the 'data', it would have been possible systematically to collect and analyse the views of those who had undertaken the experiment and see what sort of conclusions were forthcoming. It would be possible to frame the process into a more formal experiment (perhaps of a laddering type) within a theoretical framework, with hypotheses and with accountable conclusions about the fate of the hypotheses. But perhaps the most important 'result' of this kind of venture is that it may make us look in new directions, without being too desperate to freeze what we see into a technology.

But curiously enough, if we make technology truly our technique and not our framework, then just as we can make the complex mathematics of grid method serve the expression of the individual, so we can make the overweight expertise of the computer serve the purposes of McFall's Mystical Monitor. Thomas (1970) is developing ways in which a man may talk to himself, using as his sounding board the language of repertory grid technique programmed into a computer. The 'subject' (the problem of who is running the show and on whose behalf it is all being undertaken arises yet again) sits down at the computer, which begins to ask him questions about how his bookie and his wife are alike and thereby different from his boss. The person goes on 'telling' the computer his views of people in his world (or his differential evaluations of wines or films or towns or computer programmes). The computer stores and analyses this information and feeds the results of the analysis to the 'subject'. Thus the person is now not simply hearing what he said, but having some of the implications of what he said worked out for him. He may be told what the relationships between his constructs are, or which people he seems to have great difficulty in understanding. (A grid analysis reveals the pattern of combinations of qualities which a person sees as going together and it is therefore easy to see which people in his world are 'psychological impossibilities' – they are alleged to possess a combination of qualities contrary to the pattern, being, say, selfish and generous, clever and idiotic.) Eventually the computer may offer choice points. The subject can decide whether he wants to go on and define more

clearly a familiar part of his world or try to sort out some
new aspects of his life (the 'extension or definition' of the
choice corollary).

Again, we are faced with the problem of what are the
'results' of this kind of experiment? If the person chooses not
to wipe out the record of his transactions with the computer,
then certainly there is quantified data in abundance and
from it we might discover much about the process of construing in *real time* terms. For example, we might learn
something on that very issue of why do we sometimes choose
to define and at other times opt to extend our understanding.
But again, perhaps the most important immediate implications of this line of research have to do with the level at
which it lets the person work and the level at which we try to
understand what the person has been doing.

These are lines of experimenting with a single person, but
what of people experimenting with each other? Mair (1970a
and 1970b) has suggested that instead of using a physics
model to guide us in designing experiments, we look to the
technique which people most often use to investigate and
experiment with each other – the conversation. He suggests
that we might design experiments on a conversational
model. These might take the form of a kind of cycle of
inquiry such as he describes in the following passage.

Consider a practical situation. Mr Rogers and Mr Skinner sit
down together to undertake an exploratory study of how they
each and together 'theorize' and 'experiment' about themselves,
each other and others in general. Mr Skinner writes *two* brief
character sketches of Mr Rogers (following, perhaps, similar instructions to those used by Kelly for Self-Characterizations).
One of these sketches is written *only for himself*; a completely
private view of Mr Rogers which no one else will see. The other
sketch is written *specifically for* Mr Rogers to read. This latter
one is couched in terms and touches on topics which Mr Skinner
will feel *quite comfortable* about telling Mr Rogers, he is not
required to 'bare his soul' or 'tell all', but just to give a picture of
his view of Mr Rogers which he will feel quite able to take (one
participant must not traumatize the other or others since each

needs everyone else to stay around so that the inquiry can continue).

Mr Rogers also writes two equivalent sketches about Mr Skinner, one private for his own eyes only and the other a more public one specifically for Mr Skinner to read.

Messrs Skinner and Rogers now *pass to the other* their 'public' sketches. They read them, then systematically take turns at questioning the other to clarify points in the sketch they received which they understood little or not at all. They then take time to *note down* their initial reactions to the new information which has been given them about themselves; what they feel, think, want to do, say, reject, accept, avoid or welcome about it.

Next, in turn, each questions the other in detail about what *evidence* he has for each of the statements he has made about the other; about his grounds for believing the things he does and for saying the things he has; about the criteria he may be functioning in terms of, in accepting the evidence he has done and about the criteria and evidence he would use if he were to become more certain yet of the validity of the statements he has made. In addition, at this stage, they may then examine the description of themselves presented to them by the other and analyse it in terms of what it seems to suggest about the interests, ideas, strengths, limitations, tactics and such like *of the person who wrote it.* Each will then also take turns in questioning the other concerning the evidence which justifies the conclusions he has reached regarding the characteristics and concerns of the writer. (Here, as at any other point in the entire investigation, each may write both public and private versions of conclusions reached, the evidence he has used, the assessments he has made, and so forth.)

At this point the first face to face encounter might end and each withdraw to continue their normal lives, arranging to meet again in an hour, day, week or month (whatever their purpose in the inquiry) to continue the face to face part of the study. As they go, however, the study goes with them. In the encounter just completed many personal issues will have been touched on and stirred; each participant (and there could easily be more than two) may find, whether he wishes it or not, that he continues to ruminate on, act out, experiment with, attempt to disconfirm or confirm in a variety of imaginary or practical ways some of the issues and possibilities raised. Each participant must be vigilant to note down at any time how he goes about dealing with these matters (and this is likely to require considerable training in sensitive, detached self-awareness).

The cycle of encounter and withdrawal for personal exploration can be repeated indefinitely or terminated at any agreed stage, depending on the main point of the study or the concerns of those involved.

Looking at the suggested procedure we are faced again by the same problems (or are they solutions?) which we saw in relation to the two earlier ventures. Who are the experimenters and who are the subjects? What about the data which by its very nature will not become public property? And where have all the statistics gone? And what about the 'results'? On the last question we can see the kind of issues on which this sort of experiment might throw light. What are we to make of any discrepancy between my portrait of you for you and my portrait of you which I feel I must keep to myself? Are we to take the barren view that it is a measure of the extent to which I lie? Or could we see it perhaps as the beginnings of a way to measure the nature of the role relationship between you and me?

And suppose – as Mair suggests – we add in other viewpoints, such as how I view myself for myself or how we view each other later, after we have been through the cycle once. Might not content analyses of yet further differences between these viewpoints reveal something about the ways in which we go about handling evidence or the degree to which others can see us in our own terms?

Pondering the question of 'results' inevitably leads us to the interesting construct of replicability, for psychologists talk much of replication and revere it as a defining characteristic of science. What does replicability mean in experimental psychology? It does not mean that there is any likelihood that our experiments will be exactly repeated, for this is a fantastically rare event. It seems to mean that we have designed and presented them in such a way that they *could* be repeated. Presumably this is not for some tricksy reason such as reassuring others that we have not lied about our results because we would not be so foolish, knowing they could be checked upon. It seems more likely that replicability is a discipline we impose upon ourselves to make sure that the way we have defined our experimental operations is clear enough to communicate itself reliably to other psychologists.

This is fine, but let us acknowledge that what is thereby rendered relatively indisputable is the *operational procedures* of the experiment. The theoretical argument, that which the whole experiment was about, may still be painfully vague. There may be no real agreement about what it all means, only a disagreement concealed by our happy unity about the definition of the operational procedures. We may be agreed as to what we mean by the rate of shitting in the rat, we may even be agreed that we will refer to this as an operational definition of 'emotionality', but we have not thereby come to any sort of agreement as to what, in the long run and in all its glory, 'emotionality' is going to be taken to mean. In terms of this kind of view of replicability, are the kinds of experiment foreshadowed by the conversational model procedures likely to prove susceptible to 'replication'? If a large number of experimenters undertake such procedures (giving us genuine multiple replication), then they can state the conclusions they have drawn in formal and general terms. If we find identifiable themes repeated in these conclusions, we may be able to examine them by alternative procedures in new contexts. Then may we not have achieved the kind of commonality and basis for useful ongoing scientific argument that is normally sought for the rubric of replicability? Certainly it would be better to find the answer to such a question by conducting experiments of this kind, rather than ignoring them because they do not fit the narrowest possible interpretation put on the science club rules.

A perspective for psychology

There is evidence that pure data-grubbing and common sense eclecticism are already diminishing styles in psychology, though the need for quick pay-offs in applied fields may maintain these traditions for a while longer. Most psychologists seem to be moving on from accepting Popper's dictum about the need for our hypotheses to be falsifiable to accepting his more extensive definition of science as essentially a line of argument – and a line of argument needs an integrated language if it is not to be continually derailed. Theory is a necessary *basis* for scientific endeavour, not the end product of fact-gathering or icing to be added when the real business of cake-baking is over. Popper discussed this in the following terms:

Thus the real situation is quite different from the one visualized by the naïve empiricist, or the believer in inductive logic. He thinks that we begin by collecting and arranging our experiences, and so ascend the ladder of science. Or to use the more formal mode of speech, that if we wish to build up a science, we have first to collect protocol sentences. But if I am ordered: 'record what you are now experiencing' I shall hardly know how to obey this ambiguous order. Am I to report that I am writing: that I hear a bell ringing: a newsboy shouting: a loud-speaker droning: or am I to report, perhaps, that these noises irritate me? And even if the order could be obeyed: however rich a collection of statements might be assembled in this way, it could never add up to a *science*. A science needs points of view and theoretical problems (Popper, 1959).

In passing we might note that Popper's picture of scientists as proceeding by refuting their own conjectures is quite a neat description, from a construct theory viewpoint, of how we extend our personal lives.

But a further necessary development in our perspective of a science of psychology has to do with questions such as how does a science of psychology relate to our personal psychologies? What of the value problems implicit in trying to develop a science of psychology? What are the limits of detachment and objectivity? Can psychologists cite curiosity as the grounds for their proceedings or is this to understate their committal to their subject? These are questions which psychologists seem rarely to consider.

The aim of science is conventionally stated to be prediction and control. The aim of a psychology of personal constructs, put at its most pious, is liberation through understanding. A construct theorist sees prediction not as an aim, but as a means of putting our understanding to the test. Control, in any complete sense, is not an aim but a dangerous myth.

Appendix
Formal content of personal construct theory

fundamental postulate A person's processes are psychologically channellized by the ways in which he anticipates events.

construction corollary A person anticipates events by construing their replications.

individuality corollary Persons differ from each other in their constructions of events.

organization corollary Each person characteristically evolves for his convenience in anticipating events, a construction system embracing ordinal relationships between constructs.

dichotomy corollary A person's construction system is composed of a finite number of dichotomous constructs.

choice corollary A person chooses for himself that alternative in a dichotomized construct through which he anticipates the greatest possibility for the elaboration of his system.

range corollary A construct is convenient for the anticipation of a finite range of events only.

experience corollary A person's construction system varies as he successively construes the replications of events.

modulation corollary The variation in a person's construction system is limited by the permeability of the constructs within whose range of convenience the variants lie.

fragmentation corollary A person may successively employ a variety of construction systems which are inferentially incompatible with each other.

commonality corollary To the extent that one person employs a construction of experience which is similar to that employed by another, his processes are psychologically similar to those of the other person.

sociality corollary To the extent that one person construes the construction process of another he may play a role in a social process involving the other person.

Formal aspects of constructs

range of convenience A construct's range of convenience comprises all those things to which the user would find its application useful.

focus of convenience A construct's focus of convenience comprises those particular things to which the user would find its application maximally useful. These are the elements upon which the construct is likely to have been formed originally.

elements The things or events which are abstracted by a person's use of a construct are called elements. In some systems these are called objects.

context The context of a construct comprises those elements among which the user ordinarily discriminates by means of the construct. It is somewhat more restricted than the range of convenience, since it refers to the circumstances in which the construct emerges for practical use and not necessarily to all the circumstances in which a person might eventually use the construct. It is somewhat more extensive than the focus of convenience, since the construct may often appear in circumstances where its application is not optimal.

pole Each construct discriminates between two poles, one at each end of its dichotomy. The elements abstracted are like each other at each pole with respect to the construct and are unlike the elements at the other pole.

contrast The relationship between the two poles of a construct is one of contrast.

likeness end When referring specifically to elements at one pole of a construct, one may use the term 'likeness end' to designate that pole.

contrast end When referring specifically to elements at one pole of a construct, one may use the term 'contrast end' to designate the opposite pole.

emergence The emergent pole of a construct is that one which embraces most of the immediately perceived context.

implicitness The implicit pole of a construct is that one which embraces contrasting context. It contrasts with the emergent pole. Frequently the person has no available symbol or name for it; it is symbolized only implicitly by the emergent term.

symbol An element in the context of a construct which represents not only itself but also the construct by which it is abstracted by the user is called the construct's symbol.

permeability A construct is permeable if it admits newly perceived elements to its context. It is impermeable if it rejects elements on the basis of their newness.

Constructs classified according to the nature of their control over their elements

preemptive construct A construct which preempts its elements for membership in its own realm exclusively is called a preemptive construct. This is the 'nothing but' type of construction – 'if this is a ball it is nothing but a ball'.

constellatory construct A construct which fixes the other realm membership of its elements is called a constellatory construct. This is stereotyped or typological thinking.

propositional construct A construct which carries no implications regarding the other realm membership of its elements is a propositional construct. This is uncontaminated construction.

General diagnostic constructs

preverbal constructs A preverbal construct is one which continues to be used, even though it has no consistent word symbol. It may or may not have been devised before the client had command of speech symbolism.

submergence The submerged pole of a construct is the one which is less available for application to events.

suspension A suspended element is one which is omitted from the context of a construct as a result of revision of the client's construct system.

level of cognitive awareness The level of cognitive awareness ranges from high to low. A high-level construct is one which is readily expressed in socially effective symbols; whose alternatives are both readily accessible; which falls well within the range of convenience of the client's major construction; and which is not suspended by its superordinating constructs.

dilation Dilation occurs when a person broadens his perceptual field in order to reorganize it on a more comprehensive level. It does not, in itself, include the comprehensive reconstruction of those elements.

constriction Constriction occurs when a person narrows his perceptual field in order to minimize apparent incompatibilities.

comprehensive constructs A comprehensive construct is one which subsumes a wide variety of events.

incidental constructs An incidental construct is one which subsumes a narrow variety of events.

superordinate constructs A superordinate construct is one which includes another as one of the elements in its context.

subordinate constructs A subordinate construct is one which is included as an element in the context of another.

regnant constructs A regnant construct is a kind of superordinate construct which assigns each of its elements to a category on an all-or-none basis, as in classical logic. It tends to be non-abstractive.

core constructs A core construct is one which governs a person's maintenance processes.

peripheral constructs A peripheral construct is one which can be altered without serious modification of the core structure.

tight constructs A tight construct is one which leads to unvarying predictions.

loose constructs A loose construct is one which leads to varying predictions but which retains its identity.

Constructs relating to transition

threat Threat is the awareness of an imminent comprehensive change in one's core structures.

fear Fear is the awareness of an imminent incidental change in one's core structures.

anxiety Anxiety is the awareness that the events with which one is confronted lie mostly outside the range of convenience of one's construct system.

guilt Guilt is the awareness of dislodgement of the self from one's core role structure.

aggressiveness Aggressiveness is the active elaboration of one's perceptual field.

hostility Hostility is the continued effort to exort validational evidence in favour of a type of social prediction which has already been recognized as a failure.

cpc cycle The CPC Cycle is a sequence of construction involving in succession, circumspection, preemption, and control, leading to a choice precipitating the person into a particular situation.

creativity cycle The Creativity Cycle is one which starts with loosened construction and terminates with tightened and validation construction.

References

ADAMS-WEBBER, J. R. (1969), 'Cognitive complexity and sociality', *Brit. J. soc. clin. Psychol.*, vol. 8, pp. 211–16.

ALLPORT, G. W. (1937), *Personality: A Psychological Interpretation*, Holt, Rinehart & Winston.

ALLPORT, G. W. (1964), 'The fruits of eclecticism – bitter or sweet?', *Acta Psychol.*, vol. 23, pp. 27–44.

ARGYLE, M. (1969), *Social Interaction*, Methuen.

ARGYLE, M., SALTER, V., NICHOLSON, H., WILLIAMS, M., and BURGESS, P. (1970), 'The communication of inferior and superior attitudes by verbal and non-verbal signals', *Brit. J. soc. clin. Psychol.*, vol. 9, pp. 222–31.

ARGYRIS, C. (1969), 'The incompleteness of social-psychological theory: examples from small group, cognitive consistency and attribution research', *Amer. Psychol.*, vol. 24, pp. 893–908.

ASCH, S. E. (1951), 'Effects of group pressure upon the modification and distortion of judgment', in H. Guetzkow (ed.), *Groups, Leadership and Men*, Carnegie Press.

ASCH, S. E. (1956), 'Studies of independence and conformity: a minority of one against a unanimous majority', *Psychol. Monogrs.*, vol. 70, no. 9 (whole no. 416).

BAKAN, D. (1954), 'A generalisation of Sidman's results on group and individual functions, and a criterion', *Psychol. Bull.*, vol. 51, pp. 63–4.

BALOFF, N., and BECKER, S. W. (1967), 'On the futility of aggregating individual learning curves', *Psychol. Reports*, vol. 20, pp. 183–91.

BANNISTER, D. (1959), 'An application of personal construct theory (Kelly) to schizoid thinking', unpublished Ph.D. thesis, London University.

BANNISTER, D. (1960), 'Conceptual structure in thought-disordered schizophrenics', *J. ment. Sci.*, vol. 106, pp. 1230–49.

BANNISTER, D. (1962a), 'The nature and measurement of schizophrenic thought disorder', *J. ment. Sci.*, vol. 108, pp. 825–42.

BANNISTER, D. (1962b), 'Personal construct theory: a summary and experimental paradigm', *Acta Psychol.*, vol. 20, no. 2, pp. 104–20.

BANNISTER, D. (1963), 'The genesis of schizophrenic thought disorder: a serial invalidation hypothesis', *Brit. J. Psychiat.*, vol. 109, p. 680.

BANNISTER, D. (1965), 'The genesis of schizophrenic thought disorder: re-test of the serial invalidation hypothesis', *Brit. J. Psychiat.*, vol. 111, p. 377.

BANNISTER, D. (1966a), 'Psychology as an exercise in paradox', *Bull. Brit. Psychol. Soc.*, vol. 19, pp. 21–6.

BANNISTER, D. (1966b), 'A new theory of personality', in B. Foss (ed.), *New Horizons in Psychology*, Penguin.

BANNISTER, D. (1968), 'The myth of physiological psychology', *Bull. Brit. Psychol. Soc.*, vol. 21, pp. 229–31.

BANNISTER, D. (1970a), 'Science through the looking glass', in D. Bannister (ed.), *Perspectives in Personal Construct Theory*, Academic Press.

BANNISTER, D. (1970b), 'Psychological theories as ways of relating to people', *Brit. J. med. Psychol.*, vol. 43, pp. 241–4.

BANNISTER, D. (1970c), 'Comment on explanation and the concept of personality', in R. Borger and F. Cioffi (eds.), *Explanation in the Behavioural Sciences*, Cambridge University Press.

BANNISTER, D., and BOTT, M. (1971), personal communication.

BANNISTER, D., and FRANSELLA, F. (1966), 'A grid test of schizophrenic thought disorder', *Brit. J. soc. clin. Psychol.*, vol. 5, pp. 95–102. Also in Psychological Test Publications, Barnstaple (1967).

BANNISTER, D., FRANSELLA, F., and AGNEW, J. (1971), 'Characteristics and validity of the grid test of thought disorder', *Brit. J. soc. clin. Psychol.*, vol. 10, pp. 144–51.

BANNISTER, D., and MAIR, J. M. M. (1968), *The Evaluation of Personal Constructs*, Academic Press.

BANNISTER, D., and SALMON, P. (1966), 'Schizophrenic thought disorder: specific or diffuse?', *Brit. J. med. Psychol.*, vol. 39, pp. 215–19.

BARBER, T., and SILVER, M. J. (1968), 'Fact, fiction and the experimenter bias effect', *Psychol. Bull.*, vol. 70, no. 6, part 2, monograph supplement.

BARTLETT, F. C. (1932), *Remembering*, Cambridge University Press.

BATESON, G., JACKSON, D., HALEY, J., and WEAKLAND, J. (1956), 'Towards a theory of schizophrenia', *Behavioural Science*, vol. 4.

BEECH, H. R., and FRANSELLA, F. (1968), *Research and Experiment in Stuttering*, Pergamon Press.

BENDER, M. P. (1968), 'Does construing people as similar involve similar behaviour towards them?', *Brit. J. soc. clin. Psychol.*, vol. 7, pp. 303–4.

BERNSTEIN, B. (1959), 'A public language: some sociological implications of a linguistic form', *Brit. J. Sociol.*, vol. 10, pp. 311–26.

BERNSTEIN, B. (1961), 'Social class and linguistic development: a theory of social learning' in A. H. Halsey, J. Floud and A. C. Anderson (eds.), *Education, Economy and Society*, Free Press.

BIERI, J. (1966), 'Cognitive and complexity and personality development', in O. J. Harvey (ed.), *Experience, Structure and Adaptability*. Springer, New York.

BILLS, A. G. (1938), 'Changing views of psychology as a science', *Psychol. Rev.*, vol. 45, pp. 377–94.

BONARIUS, J. C. J. (1965), 'Research in the personal construct theory of George A. Kelly: role construct repertory test and basic theory', in B. Maher (ed.), *Progress in Experimental Personality Research*, vol. 2. Academic Press.

BONARIUS, J. C. J. (1970), 'Fixed role therapy: a double paradox', *Brit. J. med. Psychol.*, vol. 43, pp. 213–19.

BORING, E. G. (1929), 'The psychology of controversy', *Psychol. Rev.*, vol. 36, pp. 97–121.

BORING, E. G. (1950), *History of Experimental Psychology*, 2nd edn, Appleton–Century–Crofts.

BORGATTA, E. F., and BALES, R. F. (1953), 'Interaction of individuals in reconstituted groups', *Sociometry*, vol. 16, pp. 327–38.

BRIERLEY, D. W. (1967), 'The use of personality constructs by children of three different ages', unpublished Ph.D. thesis, London University.

BROWN, J. A. C. (1963), *Techniques of Persuasion*, Penguin Books.

BRUNER, J. S. (1956), 'You are your constructs', *Contemp. Psychol.*, vol. 1, pp. 355–7.

BURGESS, R. (1968), 'Communication networks: an experimental re-evaluation', *J. exp. soc. Psychol.*, vol. 4, pp. 324–37.

CAINE, T. M., and SMAIL, D. J. (1969a), *The Treatment of Mental Illness: Science, Faith and the Therapeutic Personality*, University of London Press.

CAINE, T. M., and SMAIL, D. J. (1969b), 'The effects of personality and training on attitudes to treatment: preliminary investigations', *Brit. J. med. Psychol.*, vol. 42, pp. 277–82.

CANTER, D. (1970), 'Individual response to the physical environment', *Bull. Brit. Psychol. Soc.* (abstract), vol. 23, p. 123.

CARTWRIGHT, R. D., and LERNER, B. (1963), 'Empathy, need to change, and improvement with psychotherapy', *J. Consult. Psychol.*, vol. 27, pp. 138–44.

CHAPANIS, N. P., and CHAPANIS, A. (1964), 'Cognitive dissonance: five years later', *Psychol. Bull.*, vol. 61, pp. 1–22.

COX, C. B., and DYSON, A. E. (1969), *Fight For Education: A Black Paper*, Critical Quarterly Society.

DEESE, J. (1969), 'Behavior and fact', *Amer. Psychol.*, vol. 24, pp. 515–22.

DEUTSCH, M., and COLLINS, M. (1951), *Inter-racial Housing: A Psychological Evaluation of a Social Experiment*, University of Minnesota Press.

DOLLIVER, R. H. (1969), 'Strong vocational interest blank versus expressed vocational interests: a review', *Psychol. Bull.*, vol. 72, pp. 95–107.

DREWERY, J., and RAE, J. B. (1969), 'A group comparison of alcoholic and non-alcoholic marriages using the interpersonal perception technique', *Brit. J. Psychiat.*, vol. 115, pp. 287–300.

DU MAS, F. M. (1955), 'Science and the single case', *Psychol. Reps.*, vol. 1, pp. 65–75.

FESTINGER, L. (1957), *A Theory of Cognitive Dissonance*, Row, Peterson.

FOULDS, G. A., HOPE, K., McPHERSON, F. M., and MAYO, P. R. (1967), 'Cognitive disorder among the schizophrenias. 1: The validity of some tests of thought-process disorder', *Brit. J. Psychiat.*, vol. 113, pp. 1361–8.

FRANSELLA, F. (1965), 'The effects of imposed rhythm and certain aspects of personality on the speech of stutterers', unpublished Ph.D. thesis, London University.

FRANSELLA, F. (1968), 'Self concepts and the stutterer', *Brit. J. Psychiat.*, vol. 114, pp. 1531–5.

FRANSELLA, F. (1969), 'The stutterer as subject or object', in B. B. Gray and G. England (eds.), *Stuttering and the Conditioning Therapies*, Monterey Institute of Speech and Hearing, California.

FRANSELLA, F. (1970a), 'Stuttering: not a symptom but a way of life', *Brit. J. Disord. Communic.*, vol. 5, pp. 22–9.

FRANSELLA, F. (1970b), '. . . And then there was one', in D. Bannister (ed.), *Perspectives in Personal Construct Theory*, Academic Press.

FRANSELLA, F. (1970c), 'Construing and the dysphasic', unpublished MS.

FRANSELLA, F. (1970d), 'Measurement of conceptual change accompanying weight loss', *J. psychosom. Res.*, vol. 14, pp. 347–51.

FRANSELLA, F. (1971a), *Personal Construct Psychotherapy and Stuttering*, Academic Press, in press.

FRANSELLA, F. (1971b), 'A personal construct theory and treatment of stuttering', *J. psychosom. Res.*, in press.

FRANSELLA, F., and ADAMS, B. (1966), 'An illustration of the use of repertory grid technique in a clinical setting', *Brit. J. soc. clin. Psychol.*, vol. 5, pp. 51–62.

FRANSELLA, F., and BANNISTER, D. (1967), 'A validation of repertory grid technique as a measure of political construing', *Acta Psychol.*, vol. 26, pp. 97–106.

FRANSELLA, F., and CRISP, A. H. (1971), 'Conceptual organization and weight change', *J. psychosom. Res.*, in press.

FRANSELLA, F., and JOYSTON-BECHAL, M. P. (1971), 'An investigation of conceptual process and pattern change in a psychotherapy group over one year', *Brit. J. Psychiat.*, vol. 119, pp. 199–206.

FRIEDMAN, H. J. (1966), 'Patient-expectancy and symptom reduction', in A. P. Goldstein and S. J. Dean (eds.), *Investigation of Psychotherapy*, Wiley, pp. 311–18.

GEIWITZ, P. J. (1969), *Non-Freudian Personality Theories*, Brooks-Cole.

GOLD, M. (1969), 'Juvenile delinquency as a symptom of alienation', *J. soc. Issues*, vol. 25, pp. 121–35.

HALL, C. S., and LINDZEY, G. (1957), *Theories of Personality*, Wiley.

HARTSHORNE, H., and MAY, M. (1928), *Studies in the Nature of Character*, Vol. I, Macmillan.

HINKLE, D. N. (1965), 'The change of personal contructs from the viewpoint of a theory of implications', unpublished Ph.D. thesis, Ohio State University.

HOFFMAN, D. T., SCHACKNER, R., and GOLDBLATT, R. (1970), '"Friendliness" of the experimenter', *Psychol. Rec.*, vol. 20, pp. 41–4.

HOLLAND, R. (1970), 'George Kelly: constructive innocent and reluctant existentialist', in D. Bannister (ed.), *Perspectives in Personal Construct Theory*, Academic Press.

HOLLAND, S. (1971), 'Perceived powerlessness of self and others among delinquents', unpublished MA thesis, London University.

HOWARD, J. W. (1970), 'Management – power and independence', unpublished MS.

HUDSON, L. (1968), *Contrary Imaginations*, Penguin Books.

HUDSON, L. (1970), *Frames of Mind*, Penguin Books.

HUMPHREY, G. (1933), *The Nature of Learning*, Harcourt, Brace & World.

JAMES, W. (1891), *Principles of Psychology*, vol. 1, Macmillan, p. 16.

JOHNSON, W. (1942), 'A study of the onset and development of stuttering', *J. Speech Disord.*, vol. 7, pp. 251–7.

JOHNSON, R. P. (1969), 'Some observations of the behaviour of woodlice (oniscus asellus) in a magnetic field', *Bull. Brit. Soc. Psychol.* (abstract), vol. 22, p. 215.

KARST, T. O., and TREXLER, L. D. (1970), 'Initial study using fixed-role and rational-emotive therapy in treating public-speaking anxiety', *J. consult. clin. Psychol.*, vol. 34, pp. 360–66.

KELLEY, H. H. (1950), 'The warm–cold variable in first impressions', *J. Person.*, vol. 18, pp. 431–9.

KELLY, G. A. (1955), *The Psychology of Personal Constructs*, vols. 1 and 2, Norton.

KELLY, G. A. (1961a), 'The abstraction of human processes', *Proceedings of the Fourteenth International Congress of Applied Psychology*, Munksgaard, Copenhagen.

KELLY, G. A. (1961b), 'Suicide: the personal construct point of view', in N. L. Farberow and E. S. Shneidman (eds.), *The Cry for Help*, McGraw-Hill.

KELLY, G. A. (1962), 'Europe's matrix of decision', in M. R. Jones (ed.), *Nebraska Symposium*, University of Nebraska Press.

KELLY, G. A. (1965), personal communication.

KELLY, G. A. (1966a), transcript of a tape-recorded conversation with F. Fransella.

KELLY, G. A. (1966b), 'The psychology of the unknown', unpublished MS.

KELLY, G. A. (1969), 'Personal construct theory and the psychotherapeutic interview', in B. Maher (ed.), *Clinical Psychology and Personality*, Wiley, pp. 224–64.

KELLY, G. A. (1970a), 'A brief introduction to personal construct theory', in D. Bannister (ed.), *Perspectives in Personal Construct Theory*, Academic Press.

KELLY, G. A. (1970b), 'Behaviour is an experiment', in D. Bannister (ed.), *Perspectives in Personal Construct Theory*, Academic Press.

KELMAN, H. C. (1967), 'Human use of human subjects: the problem of deception in social psychological experiments', *Psychol. Bull.*, vol. 67, pp. 1–11.

KENNEDY, J. J. (1969), 'Experimenter outcome bias in verbal conditioning: a failure to detect the Rosenthal effect', *Psychol. Repts.*, vol. 25, pp. 495–500.

KNOWLES, J. B., and PURVES, C. (1965), 'The use of repertory grid technique to assess the influence of the experimenter–subject relationship in verbal conditioning', *Bull. Brit. Psychol. Soc.*, vol. 18, p. 59.

KRECH, D., CRUTCHFIELD, R. S., and BALLACHEY, E. L. (1962), *The Individual in Society: A Textbook of Social Psychology*, McGraw-Hill.

LAING, R. D. (1967), *The Politics of Experience* and *The Bird of Paradise*, Penguin.

LAING, R. D., and ESTERSON, A. (1964), *Sanity, Madness and the Family*, Tavistock.

LANDFIELD, A. W. (1965), 'Role construct repertory test rating manual', unpublished MS.

LANDFIELD, A. W. (1971), *Personal Construct Systems in Psychotherapy*, Rand McNally.

LANDFIELD, A. W., and NAWAS, M. M. (1964), 'Psychotherapeutic improvement as a function of communication and adoption of therapist's values', *J. counsel. Psychol.*, vol. 11, pp. 336–41.

LEAVITT, H. J. (1951), 'Some effects of certain communication patterns on group performance', *J. abnorm. soc. psychol.*, vol. 46, pp. 38–50.

LEMAN, G. (1970a), 'Psychology as science fiction', unpublished MS.

LEMAN, G. (1970b), 'Words and worlds', in D. Bannister (ed.), *Perspectives in Personal Construct Theory*, Academic Press.

LESTER, D. (1968), 'Attempted suicide as a hostile act', *J. Psychol.*, vol. 68, pp. 243–8.

LESTER, D. (1969), 'Resentment and dependency in the suicidal individual', *J. gen. Psychol.*, vol. 81, pp. 137–45.

LEVINE, S. (1956), 'A further study of infantile handling and adult avoidance learning', *J. Person.*, vol. 25, pp. 70–80.

LIDZ, T. (1964), *The Family and Human Adaptation*, Hogarth.

LIFTON, R. J. (1961), *Thought Reform and the Psychology of Totalism*, Gollancz.

LITTLE, B. R. (1968), 'Factors affecting the use of psychological v. non-psychological constructs on the Rep. Test', *Bull. Brit. Psychol. Soc.*, vol. 21, no. 70, p. 34.

MAIR, J. M. M. (1964a), 'The derivation, reliability and validity of grid measures: some problems and suggestions', *Bull. Brit. Psychol. Soc.*, vol. 17, p. 55.

MAIR, J. M. M. (1964b), The concepts of reliability and validity in relation to construct theory and repertory grid technique, in N. Warren (ed.), *Brunel Construct Theory Seminar Report*, Brunel University.

MAIR, J. M. M. (1966), 'Prediction of grid scores', *Brit. J. Psychol.*, vol. 57, nos. 1 and 2, pp. 187–92.

MAIR, J. M. M. (1967), 'Some problems of repertory grid measurement. 2: The use of whole figure constructs', *Brit. J. Psychol.*, vol. 58.

MAIR, J. M. M. (1970a), 'Experimenting with individuals', *Brit. J. med. Psychol.*, vol. 43, pp. 245–56.

MAIR, J. M. M. (1970b), 'Psychologists are human too', in D. Bannister (ed.), *Perspectives in Personal Construct Theory*, Academic Press.

MAIR, J. M. M. (1970c), 'Psychological problems and cigarette smoking', *J. psychosom. Res.*, vol. 14, pp. 277–83.

MAKHLOUF-NORRIS, F. (1968), 'Concepts of the self and others in obsessional neurosis studied by an adaptation of the role construct repertory grid', unpublished Ph.D. thesis, London University.

MAKHLOUF-NORRIS, F., JONES, H. G., and NORRIS, H. (1970), 'Articulation of the conceptual structure in obsessional neurosis', *Brit. J. soc. clin. Psychol.*, vol. 9, pp. 264–74.

MARCIA, J. E., RUBIN, B. M., and EFRAN, J. S. (1969), 'Systematic desensitisation: expectancy change or counterconditioning?', *J. abnorm. Psychol.*, vol. 74, pp. 382–7.

MARKS, I., and GELDER, M. (1967), 'Transvestism and fetishism: clinical and psychological changes during faradic aversion', *Brit. J. Psychiat.*, vol. 113, pp. 711–29.

McCOMSKY, J. *et al.* (1969), 'An experimental investigation of some basic concepts in architecture', *Int. J. educ. Sci.*, vol. 3, pp. 199–208.

McFALL, R. M. (1965), personal communication.

McPHERSON, F. M., and WALTON, H. J. (1970), 'The dimensions of psychotherapy group interaction: an analysis of clinicians' constructs', *Brit. J. med. Psychol.*, vol. 43, pp. 281–90.

MILGRAM, S. (1965), 'Some conditions of obedience and disobedience to authority', *Hum. Rel.*, vol. 18, pp. 57–76.

OLIVEAU, D. C. (1969), 'Systematic desensitisation in an experimental setting: a follow-up study', *Behav. Res. Therap.*, vol. 7, pp. 377–80.

OLIVEAU, D. C., AGRAS, W. S., LEITENBERG, H., MOORE, R. C., and WRIGHT, D. E. (1969), 'Systematic desensitisation, therapeutically oriented instructions and selective positive reinforcement', *Behav. Res. Therap.*, vol. 7, pp. 27–33.

ORNE, M. T. (1959), 'The nature of hypnosis: artifact and essence', *J. abnorm. Psychol.*, vol. 58, pp. 277–99.

ORNE, M. T. (1962), 'On the social psychology of the psychological experiment: with particular reference to demand characteristics and their implications', *Amer. Psychol* , vol. 17, pp. 776–83.

OSGOOD, C. E., SUCI, G. J., and TANNENBAUM, P. M. (1957), *The Measurement of Meaning*, University of Illinois Press.

PERVIN, L. A. (1970), *Personality: Theory, Assessment and Research*, Wiley.

PIERCE, A. H. (1908), 'The subconscious again', *J. Phil., Psychol. Sci. Meth.*, vol. 5, pp. 264–71.

POPPER, K. R. (1959), *The Logic of Scientific Discovery*, Hutchinson.

RAVENETTE, A. T. (1968), *Dimensions of Reading Difficulties*, Pergamon.

RAVENETTE, A. T. (1969), 'The situations grid: a further development in grid techniques with children', unpublished MS.

RAVENETTE, A. T. (1970), 'A further development of the situations grid: use of a certainty – uncertainty dimension', unpublished MS.

RIEDEL, W. W. (1970), 'An investigation of personal constructs through non-verbal tasks', *J. abnorm. Psychol.*, vol. 76, pp. 173–9.

ROGERS, C. A. (1958), 'A process conception of psychotherapy', *Amer. Psychol.*, vol. 13, pp. 142–9.

ROLLIN, H. R. (1969), *The Mentally Abnormal Offender and the Law*, Pergamon.

ROSENTHAL, R. (1967), 'Covert communication in the psychological experiment', *Psychol. Bull.*, vol. 67, pp. 356–67.

ROSENTHAL, R., and JACOBSON, L. (1966), 'Teachers' expectancies: determinants of pupils' IQ gains', *Psychol. Repts.*, vol. 19, pp. 115–18.

ROSENTHAL, R., and JACOBSON, L. (1968), *Pygmalion in the Classroom: Teacher Expectation and Pupils' Intellectual Development*, Holt, Rinehart & Winston.

ROSENTHAL, R., KOHN, P., GREENFIELD, P. M., and CAROTA, N. (1966), 'Data desirability, experimenter expectancy, and the results of psychological research', *J. Person. soc. Psychol.* vol. 3, pp. 20–27.

ROSS, A. O. (1963), 'Deviant case analysis: neglected approach to behaviour research', *Percept. Motor Skills*, vol. 16, pp. 337–40.

RUNKEL, P. J., and DAMRIN, D. E. (1961), 'Effect of training and anxiety upon teachers' preference for information about students', *J. Educ. Psychol.*, vol. 52, pp. 354–61.

RYCHLAK, J. F. (1968), *The Philosophy of Science for Personality Theory*, Houghton Mifflin.

RYLE, A., and LUNGHI, M. E. (1969), 'The measurement of relevant change after psychotherapy: use of repertory grid testing', *Brit. J. Psychiat.*, vol. 115, pp. 1297–304.

RYLE, A., and LUNGHI, M. E. (1970), 'The dyad grid: a modification of repertory grid technique', *Brit. J. Psychiat.*, vol. 117, pp. 323–7.

SALMON, P. (1963), 'A clinical investigation of sexual identity', unpublished case study.

SALMON, P. (1969), 'Differential conforming as a developmental process', *Brit. J. soc. clin. Psychol.*, vol. 8, pp. 22–31.

SALMON, P. (1970), 'A psychology of personal growth', in D. Bannister (ed.), *Perspectives in Personal Construct Theory*, Academic Press.

SALMON, P. (1971), personal communication.

SALMON, P., and BANNISTER, D. (1969), 'Education in the light of personal construct theory', unpublished MS.

SALMON, P., BRAMLEY, J., and PRESLY, A. S. (1967), 'The word-in-context test as a measure of conceptualization in schizophrenics with and without thought disorder', *Brit. J. med. Psychol.*, vol. 40, pp. 253–9.

SECHREST, L. B. (1963), 'The psychology of personal constructs: George Kelly', in J. M. Wepman and R. W. Heine (eds.), *Concepts of Personality*, Aldine.

SECHREST, L. B., and BARGER, B. (1961), 'Verbal participation and perceived benefit from group psychotherapy', *Int. J. Gp. Psychother.*, vol. 11, pp. 49–59.

SHEIN, E. H. (1956), 'Epilogue: something new in history?', *J. soc. Issues*, vol. 13, pp. 56–60.

SIDMAN, M. (1952), 'A note on functional relations obtained from group data', *Psychol. Bull.*, vol. 49, pp. 263–9.

SLATER, P. (1964), *The Principal Components of a Repertory Grid*, Vincent Andrew.

SMAIL, D. J. (1970), 'Neurotic symptoms, personality and personal constructs', *Brit. J. Psychiat.*, vol. 117, pp. 645–8.

THOMAS, L. F. (1970), 'Kelly – McQuitty – a computer programme for use with an on-line terminal', unpublished MS.

TRIANDIS, H. C. (1959), 'Cognitive similarity and interpersonal communication in industry', *J. appl. Psychol.*, vol. 43., pp. 321–6.

TRUAX, C. B. (1961), 'The process of group psychotherapy: relationships between hypothesized therapeutic conditions and intrapersonal exploration', *Psychol. Monogrs.*, vol. 75, no. 7, pp. 1–35.

TRUAX, C. B., CARKHUFF, R. R., and KODMAN, F., Jr (1965), 'Relationships between therapist-offered conditions and patient change in group psychotherapy', *J. clin. Psychol.*, vol. 21, pp. 327–9.

TRYON, R. C. (1934), 'Individual differences', in F. A. Moss (ed.), *Comparative Psychology*, Prentice-Hall.

VERNON, P. E. (1964), *Personality Assessment: A Critical Survey*, Methuen.

VERNON, P. E. (1969), *Intelligence and Cultural Environment*, Methuen.

VINCE, MARGARET (1967), 'Respiration as a factor in communication between quail embryos', *Bull. Brit. Psychol. Soc.* (abstract), vol. 20, p. 29.

WALKER, A. M., RABLEN, R. A., and ROGERS, C. A. (1960), 'Development of a scale to measure process changes in psychotherapy', *J. clin. Psychol.*, vol. 16, pp. 79–85.

WARR, P. B., SCHRODER, H. M., and BLACKMAN, S. (1969), 'The structure of political judgment', *Brit. J. soc. clin. Psychol.*, vol. 8, pp. 32–43.

WARREN, N. (1966), 'Social class and construct systems: an examination of the cognitive structure of two social class groups', *Brit. J. soc. clin. Psychol.*, vol. 5, pp. 254–63.

WATSON, J. P. (1970), 'A repertory grid method of studying groups', *Brit. J. Psychiat.*, vol. 117, pp. 309–18.

WHORF, B. J. (1956), in J. B. Carroll (ed.), *Language, Thought and Reality: Selected Writings of Benjamin Lee Whorf*, Wiley.

WOLPE, J. (1954), 'Reciprocal inhibition as the main basis of psychotherapeutic effects', *Amer. Med. Assoc. Arch. Neurol. Psychiat.*, vol. 72, pp. 205–26.

WRIGHT, K. J. T. (1970), 'Exploring the uniqueness of common complaints', *Brit. J. med. Psychol.*, vol. 43, pp. 221–32.

Index

Penguin Science of Behaviour